THE ART OF LIVING
AND THE
50+ WOMAN

THE ART OF LIVING
AND THE
50+ WOMAN

Anne H. Adams

Library of Congress Control Number:		2006906336
ISBN:	Hardcover	9781425725273
	Softcover	9781425725266
	eBook	9781524583781

Print information available on the last page.

Rev. date: 02/13/2017

To order additional copies of this book, contact:
Xlibris
1-888-795-4274
www.Xlibris.com
Orders@Xlibris.com
34345

Contents

Part Two: People Who Can
Help Us Live Well

Part Three: The Pre-departure Lounge

TO ADAM

THE WIND BENEATH MY WINGS

INTRODUCTION

My mother's death a year ago changed the way I perceive myself. When she was alive, I was a child. Now I am in the oldest generation.

I think of myself now as living in the Pre-Departure Lounge, but I do not think of this in a negative way. It's a positive concept because it forces me to ask myself how I want to spend the rest of my life. I want to live fully and well for as long as I can or until illness strikes—and strike it will. It's happening to my friends who are older. Some of my younger friends are also fighting debilitating losses.

I am not worried about getting sick—what will be will be—but I am very concerned about how I will deal with pain or more loss. Will I be able to handle it? When I ponder that question, I glance at two quotes on the wall over my desk:

A PRAYER FOR TODAY by W. Heartsill Wilson

"This is the beginning of a new day. God has given me this day to use as I will. I can waste it—or use it for good; but what I do today is important because I am exchanging a day of my life for it! When tomorrow comes, this day will be gone forever, leaving in its place something that I have traded for it. I want it to be gain and not loss; good, and not evil; success, and not failure; in order that I shall not regret the price I have paid for it."

The other quote is from Socrates: *"An unexamined life is not worth living."*

So I know *how* I want to live my life. The question is, *am I doing it?*

I've changed. For the last ten years I volunteered as a clown making children laugh at a children's hospital. Now I ask myself, "Do I really want to get up early in the morning, take the time to put on my clown face and costume, when I could spend the afternoon with my grandchildren and make them laugh?"

I used to enjoy taking adult evening classes. Now I tell myself that I really don't want to drive at night when I can relax at home. Comfort has become more important to me. Staying in bed that extra half hour, taking time for a second cup of tea, is comforting. I enjoy the quiet, the lack of pressure. I am content. Above all I am grateful for the privilege of being healthy and having a family who are all relatively well.

So what's wrong with that? Nothing! But is this what living "fully and well" means? Is this in accordance with the quotations to live by? To me, the art of living is the highest art of all. I have met many intelligent people, even some brilliant people, but I can count on the fingers of one hand those who have truly mastered the art of living.

My mother always told me, "You can learn from everyone." Maybe she was right. Why don't I learn from the people I know? Why don't I find out how they live, and perhaps adopt one or two things that would enhance my life? If I could learn what "real women" do to survive loss and pain, maybe I can use some of their techniques when my turn comes. So I devised a series of questions that would give me answers to what I wanted to know. My questions and their answers were the genesis of this book.

I started off by asking twenty-nine women over fifty, from various backgrounds and walks of life, to tell me about themselves. After age fifty they had reached "the age of wisdom," and I wanted to know what they learned. I asked them some basic questions:

What do you know now that you did not know when you were younger?

What advice would you give to others?

What was the best advice you ever received?

What gives you pleasure?

What do you enjoy doing?

What do you look forward to?

What sustains you in difficult times?

Does religion play a role in your life?

What would you like written on your epitaph?

How would you like to be remembered?

If you meet God, what would you like Him to say to you, or what would you like to say to Him?

I also asked each woman to tell me her fantasy. Because I like to laugh, I looked for humor in their stories. I found our conversations fascinating. Each interview was a learning experience for me; each gave me the opportunity to see these women in a different light. I hope that you, the reader, will also gain insight from these "real women." I invite you to imagine yourself sitting comfortably on a sofa next to me as we listen and learn from each woman.

At the beginning of these conversations, I introduce the women with a brief description or some background information. After every woman's story, I have written some of my own reflections, and I have included a few blank lines where you may want to scribble down your own thoughts. You may want to think of this as a journal or diary.

While these twenty-nine women offer inspiration, insight, wisdom, and humor, I also thought that we could gain more practical knowledge if I included interviews with professionals who have expertise in areas that affect us after age fifty. For that reason, the second part of this book complements the first half by offering information from people who can help us in concrete ways to live well: a financial planner, computer coach, sex therapist, dentist, feng shui practitioner, physician, makeover artist, osteopath, dermatologist, psychologist, elder law attorney, weight loss motivator, personal trainer, and pharmacist.

My hope is that I will be able to digest this learning process and incorporate it in the way I live. Perhaps then there will be less of a discrepancy between what I *think* living a full life should be and the comfort and quiet of a life of leisure and reflection. Whatever the result, at least I shall have learned more about what I want to know most—The Art of Living. And I want to share this with you . . .

PART ONE

WOMEN WHO HAVE REACHED
THE AGE OF WISDOM

FIONA, THE ANTIQUE DEALER

When I am in London, my sister often takes me to an antique shop where Fiona, the owner, is helpful and charming. She is a chic socialite with streaked blonde hair. At age seventy-two Fiona looks like an Italian society lady—always smartly turned out in clothes that reflect her exceptionally good taste, such as expensively cut trousers, a silk shirt, a beautifully draped Hermes scarf, and smart leather shoes. She's about a size fourteen or sixteen, but it doesn't matter because she walks with poise and confidence. I felt sure that she would have an interesting story to tell:

As a young girl in London, I experienced the deprivations and horrors of war, so I appreciate many things that today's generation takes for granted. My sense of worth is very much of that time when simple pleasures and family values were important. My parents were supportive and loving, and I was encouraged to do creative things. I went to art school to study design. I like being unique rather than following others.

By age of thirty, I had three children and what I thought was a good marriage, until my husband ran off with my sister-in-law. To recoup I went on holiday with a friend. I was not interested in meeting anyone. A large international company had its convention at the hotel where we were staying, and one of the company directors took a shine to me. After eyeing me at the pool for several hours, he asked me for a date. He was tall, handsome but not of my religion.

He told me, "One day you are going to be my wife." We were married for thirty years until he died five years ago.

I now have a live-in boyfriend who escorts me to cultural events. When we travel together to picturesque places, we each pay our own way. He's six years younger than I, but the age difference does not bother us. He calls me his D.G. (Domestic Goddess) because I like to cook and putter around the house. I appreciate him because I feel beautiful and adored when I am with him.

I bought an antique shop years ago and still find the people who come in fascinating. Their interests and collections vary so much, and their requests can be unusual. Some people collect things in a particular color: mauve, red, or blue. A young chef comes in who has the most exquisite taste but not the pocket book to match. He invests his salary on a payment plan so that he can acquire his favorite antiques.

Another client wanted a Blackmore statue that cost 10,100 £. She did not want to spend that much, so I commissioned a similar one to be made by an Italian sculptor who charged only 1000£. When it was delivered and my client saw the huge carving of a Tahitian lady with big boobs and a pineapple, she did not want it. We then sent it to a sales room where it fetched 10,000£.

An art dealer who happens to be a homosexual visits my shop quite often. Last week he came in and told me that he had been invited to appraise some artifacts. When the hostess got up from the table to get coffee, she purposely fell. When he reached down to pick her up, she pulled him towards her and . . . . I leave it up to you to imagine what happened.

When delivering a purchase, I am sometimes invited for tea. One house in particular gave me food for thought. A large painting of the client's dog, a red-haired, mean looking chow with a purple tongue, was hanging in the living room. In the dining room, a smaller picture of the dog was on a bookcase, which contained many books about dogs. Yet she had placed miniature pictures of her children on a kitchen shelf. I learn a lot about people when I see their homes.

Purchasing at sales in old houses, country manors, or castles is exciting, and I can sometimes spot a real find at a good price. If I had to start a shop now, my selection would be quite different. I would stock porcelain and heavy-duty china for dishwashers because young people today don't want to clean silver. They are impulsive in their selections, unlike older people who collect and buy for investment.

My role models, or the people I admire, are the Bedford family, aristocrats who have a grand home in the country. To make ends meet, they opened their home to the public and started a safari park. These aristocrats have a strong family life and have conquered their financial problems in a way that is innovative.

When I'm not in my shop or out buying, I enjoy gardening, reading, traveling to interesting places, and seeing how other people live. I look forward to family gatherings and doing even more traveling. Now that I am older, I listen more to advice. I don't always take it, but when I think it through, it often saves me unnecessary headaches. In difficult times I steel myself and get on with it. I am not a religious person, but I believe in God. In times of crisis, I pray.

I would like to be remembered as a good person, honest, and willing to help others. I'd like to think I left something, perhaps inspired someone. However I will be remembered, my life has been good, and I am grateful.

I do enjoy being with Fiona, visiting her exquisite shop in the heart of London, and hearing her story. Obviously, she is a woman who practices the art of living with grace and style.

YOUR THOUGHTS:

_____

_____

_____

_____

_____

_____

ATHENA, THE ARTIST

Original, creative, and artistic people are a joy to know. I feel such excitement when I visit their homes and see how they use color and space. I admire their style. Athena's erect posture and distinguished look exude confidence and distinction. I was particularly impressed with her, not only because she is multi-talented but also because she is able to continue with her life and talent in spite of a major obstacle. Let's see how she did it.

When I was thirteen years old, I went to a camp that had an art program and a wonderful art teacher. She was so free in her approach. Camp was really the genesis of my creating art. I started off as a painter. My paintings are non-objective. They have no object—no vase, no landscape. I then evolved into printmaking and other media, and now I am a paper maker and a wildlife photographer.

At some point when I was doing silk screens, I thought it would be nice if I did them on handmade paper. Once I started to make handmade paper, it had its own life and led to my traveling to ancient villages in the Yunnan and Guizhou provinces in China to see how they made their paper.

I am active in the art world and have held many administrative positions, including national vice-president of the Artists Equity Association, the Advisory Council of the Rosenbach Museum and Library, and I have participated in many television and radio panel discussions and interview programs on art nationwide. I've had one-person and group exhibitions in museums and galleries throughout the United States and Mexico.

Three years ago I was diagnosed with wet macular degeneration. (This vision problem occurs when the retina is deprived of oxygen. New vessels form to improve the blood supply, but the new vessels are very delicate and break easily, causing bleeding and damage to surrounding tissue.) It curtails many of my activities. I still attend yearly meetings on papermaking. I still enjoy traveling to expand my work. I do photography, primarily wildlife photographs. I loved the Canadian Rockies but compared to the traveling I did before, it is not as enriching.

I still take courses in art and other subjects. I've always taken courses in something. I may not have used it afterwards, but it didn't matter if the course was interesting. I would hate to feel that I had learned everything. You come into this world knowing little and every year is a learning experience.

I am now learning to adjust to macular degeneration. I am taking up golf. I don't love it the way I loved tennis, but I'm trying. I listen to a lot more books on tape. Before I didn't have the time. I used to do a lot of administrative work, but I cannot do that any more. I used to help my husband. I called myself his "external office facilitator"—and now that is curtailed.

Having macular degeneration has its frustrating moments. When that happens, I move on to something that I can manage. More and more in the larger scheme of life, I'm beginning to understand that how we perceive reality colors our reality.

When people meet me and talk to me, they seldom notice that I am visually impaired. Maybe it's because I look directly at them when I speak. Helen Keller said, and it's true, "Never bend your head. Always hold it high. Look the world straight in the eye."

I can't read. I can't drive. Not being able to drive, being dependent on my husband to drive me everywhere, was a big adjustment. One day when we were about to go grocery shopping, he called out to me for the third time, "Are you ready?

"I'm ready to have an affair," I answered.

"Don't be silly dear," he said. "You don't want an affair—I would only have to drive you there and pick you up when you're finished."

Last year I went to a support group. Everyone there was elderly—as I am—but you don't think of yourself as "elderly." About thirty people were sitting in a circle. I found them interesting. You never know so much that you can't learn more, and I picked up some little gems that made my life easier. They told me about a little store that specializes in mechanical aids for sight-impaired people. I call it my FAO Schwartz store. I love the toys (mechanical aids) that I bought there, like lots of hand-held magnifiers.

My computer has its own magnifying program—and it talks to me. I listen to books on tape and other recorded media, and I enjoy writing letters. I always wanted to be a good listener, and now I have learned to listen. I don't presume to give advice to anyone. (I have four children, and they don't take my advice.) But if I were asked for advice, I'd say: Keep active intellectually and keep active physically.

I hope to be able to continue to do the things that I do, whether it involves family or work. I enjoy my family. I enjoy my work. I'm glad that my children and grandchildren live nearby. Having a healthy family brings me joy.

My husband's family was very religious. My mother-in-law tried hard to change me. I had my own opinions, and I think I was her greatest disappointment. She had three daughters-in-law, and none of us cared a whit about religion.

During difficult times, my indomitable spirit sustains me. But quite frankly, I have never been involved in any kind of tragedy, so I won't know until I've been tested. My parents lived long, my in-laws lived long, and we had a close relationship. My children are healthy, my husband is healthy, and I'm healthy except for my "little nonsense" of vision.

What would I like written on my epitaph? Only my name. I don't have any control over how I will be remembered. I just do what is best, correct, interesting. I'm considerate of others. My art won't be remembered because there are so many artists in the world, but I feel fulfilled when doing it. I'm always learning, even with macular degeneration.

The Roman philosopher Epicetus said, "What disturbs men's minds are not events but their judgments of events." When I read that, I didn't relate it to my life. When Athena, an artist, talked about being sight-impaired as "my little nonsense" and not as a tragedy, it made me think. If I am faced with a serious health problem, will I be able to see it as a blotch on the canvas of life—difficult and frustrating at times—but relatively unimportant in the larger picture?

YOUR THOUGHTS:

_____

_____

_____

_____

_____

_____

PASQUINA, THE HAIRDRESSER

A doctor once told me that when she retires she would like to be a hairdresser or a bartender. "Why?" I asked. "Because I always wanted to be a psychologist, and these are two professions where people tell you their troubles." This is why I decided to interview Pasquina—a tall, erect hairdresser with a thick mane of unruly auburn hair—to find out what she learned from life and what kinds of problems people tell her about.

I was born in Italy but grew up as an immigrant in Venezuela. From there I went to Canada, and then I got a contract to work in San Francisco. Later I came to Philadelphia. This was my journey, and I am still in Philadelphia.

As a young girl, I used to work at my godmother's haute couture salon in Caracas. Her clientele represented such a different world from where I was coming from, a home where everyone was very conservative and straight-laced. My godmother's salon gave me a look into a glamorous atmosphere, and that is how I started. I opened my own beauty salon in Caracas when I was only eighteen. At twenty-four I had the opportunity to work in Canada, so I sold my business and moved there. I worked illegally for about six months—then I got a contract to work at a San Francisco salon. San Francisco was a cultural shock. Many of the people working at the salon were homosexuals. What surprised me was that they were open about it and accepted. They made it easier for me to adjust to a new city and provided a listening ear whenever I needed to complain about my boyfriend.

When my contract there expired, I moved to Philadelphia. I got a position in one of the most upscale salons. I still work there. My clientele range from young professionals to society matrons. I continue with the same structure of work no matter where I am, no matter what part of the world. The work is still the same. Styles change, but women always want to look beautiful at every stage of life. My younger clients are seldom satisfied with their hair. If it's curly, they want it straight; if it's straight, they want a perm. Many of my clients are older because I am particularly good at making thinner hair look full.

The goal of a hairstylist is a satisfied client. I've learned that tact is essential. A client will show me a picture of a hairstyle that I know will be unflattering. I gently try to dissuade her, but the client is adamant—she wants that particular hairdo. After I give it to her she asks, "Be honest, what do you think of it."

I may think that the ringlets accent her aging skin and heavy jowls, but I don't say so. Experience has taught me that if I tell the raw truth, the response usually is, "Well, *I* like it." And the client leaves in a huff. I usually respond with "Everyone needs a change now and then." Next week she's back, asking for her old hairdo.

Sometimes a client who seemed to be satisfied will go to another hairdresser at the salon. It's very awkward. I would prefer that she tell me beforehand—perhaps say something like she "needs a change." This way it would not be embarrassing for both of us.

My clients in their thirties and forties usually talk about their boyfriends and the parties they attend. As their age progresses, they talk about their divorces and their children, and they talk about their illnesses, their doctors, and their grandchildren who are gifted or their grandchildren who are on drugs.

Lately I've been hearing a lot of stories about the challenges women face when their husbands retire. They deal with it in different ways. Some try to interest their husbands in new hobbies, and some may share a new hobby with them. Others give up their lifestyle and try to do most things with their husbands. That usually does not work. When husbands spend more time at home, they tend to take an interest in how the wife is managing the household, and the men offer advice on how things could be improved, which is not well received. Shopping with a husband who takes ten minutes to squeeze oranges to see if they are ripe is not a fun experience.

The women who manage to keep most of their old lifestyles are the least irritated. But others are into the payback game. One gourmet cook, whose husband loves good food, sometimes asks him in the morning what he would like for dinner. He tells her and anticipates a good meal at the end of the day. Somehow she never has the right ingredients, or something went wrong, and he winds up with a so-so dinner.

My clients don't discuss money problems with me, but when the stock market went down some of my steady customers did not come in as often. If a woman is a very special customer, I can work something out so that she doesn't spend as much. I have some wonderful clients. One client sometimes invites me to join her and her husband for an evening in New York to attend the Metropolitan Opera, which is always a thrill.

I work three days a week at the salon. On the other two or three days, I freelance. My favorite freelance job is doing hairdos for weddings because everybody is so happy and so beautiful. The time goes by very fast, and I enjoy every moment.

From my experience in life and with people, I would give this advice: "Be honest with yourself. That goes for life or the way you want to look." If a woman is honest with herself and realistic about her age, she will not want a hairdo that is obviously best suited for a young face. We all want to look younger, and there is nothing wrong with that. A good hairdresser works to make the client look more youthful, taking into consideration her age and lifestyle. We all need a lift and a good haircut, and flattering hair color can make you feel really great. The best advice I ever got was from a hairdresser who told me, "Stand straight"—and I do.

What I've learned about life is, "Be happy. Life is too short." For enjoyment I go ballroom dancing. I like that a lot—that and my work. I look forward to being healthy. That's the only thing I really want.

My fantasy started in my godmother's hair salon. I always wanted to be a hairdresser, and I achieved my fantasy. In difficult times I have the support of my family. We left Venezuela together, and we are still together. Religion does not play a part in my life, but spirituality, yes! I believe in God, but I don't believe in religion. I told one client that when she dies, on her tombstone should be written: "Here is the lady who loved flowers." On mine, I don't know. I would like to be remembered as a good person. If I get to see God, I guess He would say, "You need to have your hair cut."

I occasionally treat myself to a hairdo by Pasquina. She gives you her undivided attention, pulling her fingers through your hair to see if it needs more conditioning, checking to see if the length is just right. When you leave the salon, you feel glamorous, beautiful, and ready for that special occasion. Now that I know Pasquina as a person, I feel closer to her and it's a different relationship. Asking questions has made me a better listener, and I always wanted to be a good listener.

YOUR THOUGHTS:

_____

_____

_____

_____

_____

_____

RUTH, THE SPIRITUAL SEEKER

So many of us have an inner hunger, a search for meaning, but few have actively sought that elusive goal. Meet Ruth, a searcher who talks about her life and her quest.

When I was young, my parents forced me to go to Hebrew school. I spent two days in class. I didn't like the teacher, and I did not like the subject. Instead of going into the classroom, I stayed outside and read books.

When we were children, my sister was always mean to me, a bully. When I told my mother, she said, "One of you has to be good."

"Why does it always have to be me?" I responded. At that time it made me angry. Now it makes me laugh.

I grew up in an Orthodox Jewish family, in a Jewish atmosphere, and I thought all religions respected life. The important part of religion for me was the holidays. The entire family would meet in one home. Our Passover meal started on our enclosed porch, and the tables were lined up through the living room, the dining room and into the kitchen. We must have had about thirty-five people. They all slept over; with the cousins and relatives sleeping on the floor, on couches, on cots. We spent the whole time eating and talking. It was fun. That, to me, was my religion.

When I grew older and entered the medical field as a lab technician, we had a Catholic patient with rheumatic fever who was pregnant. The doctor wanted to do a legal abortion because of her weak heart. Her priest came in, told her it was a sin to have an abortion, and made her leave the hospital. Eight months later she came back to the hospital, gave birth, and died. The baby had to be put up for adoption, and her husband was filled with grief and anger.

This was a big shock to me and the beginning of my spiritual quest. Sitting in the synagogue and saying Hebrew words that I did not understand was not enough for me. I started reading books on other religions.

In the hospital where I worked in 1947, I saw a doctor standing on his head after an operation. I was not shy so I asked him, "What in the world are you doing?" He told me that blood rushing to the head nourishes the brain cells, and if he stood on his head he would not become senile. Years later, my mother-in-law became senile. The first thing I did was to study with Indra Devi who lived in California. She was the first yoga teacher in the United States. I learned to stand on my head, and from there I went on to study yoga, then branched out to meditation, Feldenkrais, and now Pilates.

My first meditation retreat stands out in my mind. Six of us sat on pillows in a meditation room, with lit candles all around the room. The atmosphere was mystic, almost like being in a temple. Soft music played in the background. The teacher, Indra Devi, wore a white sari, sat on a peach-colored pillow, and taught us how to meditate.

After a while she said, "I would like you to picture in your mind that you are in a lovely room. There is a knock on the door. You open it, and there is someone you adore whom you haven't seen for a long time. You hug her and look into her eyes with much pleasure. Picture that and get in touch with your feelings."

In a few minutes she continued. "Now picture the same room with lovely music and there is a knock on the door.

You open it and there is someone whom you do not like. I want you to welcome her with open arms."

I slammed the door in her face.

Years have passed. Now I think I would have said "hello" to her—maybe even have given her a little hug—but not with enthusiasm. It's only taken me thirty-five years.

During another one-week retreat, we spent thirty minutes at a time with each person, six long hours sitting opposite each other, holding hands, looking into their eyes, and saying, "I am a person who . . ." At the end of the week, I didn't like myself or any other person. If it were not for the friend who took me there, I would have left immediately.

I later went to a wonderful place with the same friend for an eleven-day silent meditation retreat. We were awakened at 4:00 A.M. and went to the main room for meditation, followed by breakfast and an hour of walking meditation. Each day basically consisted of alternating walking and sitting meditations.

We were asked to spend one hour contributing our services to the monastery. I chose to prepare lunch. It was a wonderful experience for me—eleven totally silent people always knew when someone needed assistance. As the week progressed, we got a sense of each other. It reminded me of what animals do when they come upon a new person: they sniff. That is their way of learning about people. I found that there were some people whom I wanted to hug and get to know, and others whom I did not want to know.

I have one vivid memory of that place: I am standing in a hallway and I notice a plant with a beautiful flower, resting on a windowsill. I have such a sense of serenity that I want time to stop. Now forty years later, I still recall the flower and my feeling.

On the plane coming home from that silent retreat, I thought I was now such a deep thinker that I said to my friend, "You know, I don't know if I want to reach Nirvana." And my friend answered in her pixie voice, "You don't have to worry!"

A Buddhist ten-day silent meditation retreat in California was also interesting. When we arrived at the monastery, we were asked to sign a paper agreeing to keep ten vows. No talking, no sex, no reading, no telephone calls, no letters, no doing harm to any living creature. I don't remember them all, but the first was "do not kill any living creature," which makes sense because Buddhists believe in the sacredness of all life.

We had to sleep on mattresses on the floor. I noticed an ant nearby the first night. I said to the ant, "You can stay a bit, but if you bring your friends, you're out of here. I don't care about any vow."

Indra Devi used to tell us, "Before going to bed at night, ask yourself, "What have you done today to brighten someone's life?" I remember driving across the Benjamin Franklin Bridge at 1:00 A.M. in 1950 when the toll was twenty-five cents. I gave the toll keeper a dollar and told him to keep the change. I remember his delight, but it did more for me than it did for him. I still try to practice Indra Devi's advice.

I have read a lot about the Indian philosophers and the Sufis, and I have sort of combined all these beliefs in my mind. When I was in Japan and saw the Zen Gardens, I also included nature in my religion. Now that I am older and see couples holding hands, babies' faces, family gatherings and my granddaughter's face, that is my religion.

My husband's business placed me in many social occasions. When I was introduced to people, I used to shake hands but not look into their eyes. Now I do because I see each person as unique. I now want to touch them and learn their stories. I now look forward to meeting people. I think this change has come about through my spiritual searching. I realize that everyone has something distinctive about them, and I find them all interesting.

I do have some regrets. I would have liked to go to India and study more. If I were to give advice to others, I would say, "Form your own religion." When I go to the synagogue now, the rabbi who knows me puts out some books for me to read. I will not say prayers that I do not mean, but I do sing the Hebrew songs because I interpret them my way, and I like to be part of the congregation.

I sustain myself through music, meditation, exercise, and most of all through friends. Sadly, some have died. Some are in nursing homes and some have moved to Florida.

For my epitaph it would be fitting to write: "I'll be back." I would like to be remembered as a wonderful grandmother. And if I get to heaven, I want God to say, "I have been waiting for you. The children have been waiting for you."

It's nice to know that the spiritual journey is not without humor. Retreats, meditation, and silence seem to be key ingredients in the spiritual quest. I wonder if spiritual hunger can be satisfied in other ways . . .

YOUR THOUGHTS:

_____

_____

_____

_____

_____

_____

DEBRA, THE LIBRARIAN

I remember libraries of the past as pleasant places where people chatted quietly, skimmed through magazines, and acquired knowledge through reading. Today's library has so much more to offer, but I sometimes find it overwhelming. If I am lucky, I will find a caring librarian who will sit with me for a few minutes and show me how to find what I need. Debra, a senior librarian, is such a person. Here is how she talks about herself and her work.

I grew up in Brooklyn. Both my parents worked. My sister was older and did not want me tagging along. So after school I would spend my afternoons either at the library or the movie theatre. I always knew I was destined to be either a movie star or a librarian. Time passed. A lot happened, and I am now a librarian. Time changed me. I'm more compassionate, I have more patience. I think that I have more of a feeling for people. Life does not turn out the way you expect, and you just have to roll with the punches and make the best of what you have. What you expect at age thirty is not necessarily what you get when you are fifty or older. But I'm an eternal optimist. When something goes wrong with my life, I always look at someone who has more problems.

As a librarian, people often tell me their problems. If they are diagnosed with a medical condition, they sometimes go to the library to find out more information, ask where they can find it, and this leads to talking about their concerns.

What makes my job rewarding is the human interest, the people I meet whom I can help. For example, an elderly, distinguished, well-dressed man came into the library one day. He was hard of hearing and talked very loudly. He told me that his doctor told him that at his age—eighty-six—he had to be circumcised. Rather than falling off my chair, I guided him over to the other side of the room because half the room had overheard this and begun to laugh. Apparently he had some sort of reoccurring precancerous infection. He had no one to talk to, no one to turn for help, and he did not trust his doctor. But he knew enough to come to the library and ask for information. I told him to find a doctor he could communicate with and to get a second opinion.

Then this elegant, professional looking man told me that he had tied his wife to the bed. I gulped and asked why. "Because my wife has Alzheimer's," he said, "and I'm afraid to leave her alone because she could wander away or even set fire to the house."

I told him about social service agencies that could help him find somebody to take care of his wife so that he would not have to tie her to the bed whenever he left their house. It was hard for me to believe that even though this man had had a distinguished career, he had absolutely no knowledge of the services available to him and his wife. Doctors give medical advice, but some will not always recommend the right social agency. A doctor may suggest calling a national foundation but not the specific, appropriate local organization. That's where we librarians can be helpful.

The next person who walked up to my desk was a young man who had come up with a candy that he wanted to sell to gourmet food stores, but he did not know how to proceed. I showed him where he could find chocolate manufacturers and how to find somebody to advise him on a possible candy-making machine. Then he had to consider packaging, state laws and regulations, writing a business plan, getting a loan from a bank, etc. I helped him find useful information to get him started. Now whenever I go into a candy store and see his candy on display, I feel I had a small role in his success.

Librarians are also approached by a lot of soon-to-be divorced wives whose husbands are in the process of leaving them. They have no idea what to do. Interestingly enough, those who know absolutely nothing are usually lawyers' wives. I think this may be because they've left all financial decisions up to their lawyer husbands. These women often feel that they have no power to go against their husbands because they are lawyers. But there are laws that protect women during a divorce and steps they can take—and that is where the librarian helps them find the information.

We meet some women who are abused and need information on how to get help. They use our computers because they don't want their husbands to trace their calls, and their computer at home can be accessed. They even use our telephones sometimes because cell phone calls can be traced.

Almost every day someone comes in who needs information—from how to prepare a resume to which income tax form to file—but knowledge is not just found by going to a shelf and taking out a book. If you really need help, find a good librarian who can see the larger picture, one who is also willing to step out of the impersonal role. Not everyone wants to assume the personal responsibility. If you can find one that does, you are lucky. In this age of information and computers, there is less personal help. It's hard to find a librarian who has the time to go out of her way to give personal help.

When I first became a librarian I looked forward to reading a lot of books. But with all the responsibilities of my job, management, administrative duties, and making sure the computers are updated, free time to enjoy books is limited. You asked me about myself, and here I am going on and on about the library—I guess that shows how big a part of my life it is. What gets me up in the morning is knowing I have a job to do and responsibilities. I love my job and look forward to coming to work. I like reading, crossword puzzles, and ice-skating. I look forward to having more time to read and taking courses in gourmet cooking.

Do I have a fantasy? I hadn't really thought about it. Let's see, what would it be? Kidnapping Robert Redfern and going off on an island with him—with a lot of books, of course. For me life is real, not a fantasy. My child has a mental illness, and this has changed my life completely. My husband and I are responsible for our son, a responsibility that we will probably have for the rest of our lives. I'm still trying to deal with it after many years. We're lucky to live in a city where there's a wide choice of excellent psychiatrists, and we got good care for our son. The best advice I received was from a friend who said, "Love him. Don't judge him." That advice helped improve our relationship with him.

Religion does not play a role in my life. I rely on myself and believe that I'm strong and can get through things. "Never let them break your spirit" is what some movie star's mother told her daughter. I think it's good advice. For my epitaph I would like these words: "She loved people. She loved knowledge." I want to be remembered as a good mother, a good wife, and a good librarian.

This interview was an eye-opener for me. I had no idea that the library had so much to offer or that a knowledgeable, caring librarian could be so helpful. The question, of course, is whether you can find such a librarian. And if you do, you may discover a unique human being like Debra with a personal story that goes beyond book knowledge.

YOUR THOUGHTS:

_____

_____

_____

_____

_____

_____

ELIZABETH, THE FASHION STYLIST

She's fun, she's fabulous and she's fifty-plus. When I visit London, she takes me to antique shops, art galleries, funky boutiques, and the theatre. She has a wonderful eye for detail, and when I'm with her I see things through her eyes. She makes a big fuss over me, insists on taking me shopping and, as a special treat, to a posh restaurant for English High Tea. If I tell her,"but I'm not dressed," (My usual shopping outfit is a warm sweater, baggy pants, and comfortable shoes.) she says, "Who cares? I want you to enjoy yourself." I absolutely adore her—and why shouldn't I—she's my sister. Here's how Elizabeth describes herself and her work:

A creative person is one who sees and is inspired, who sees the world in other forms and colors—and that is me. Creativity is the most exciting thing in the world. It's my inspiration and motivation for creating new and exciting things. Inspiration comes in many forms. It can be a hat in a shop window, the colors of a poster, or a child's face.

All creative people are influenced by the old masters, whether it's a jewelry designer or a dress designer. Elizabeth Gage is a jewelry designer who has based most of her collection around the works of old masters. Vivian Westwood, one of the most influential and directional designers, has created much of her collection based on the images of Boucher and Gainsborough and other romantic artists. Even interior designers and architects often refer to the old masters to see the combination of colors and design.

I started off in Montreal as a fashion stylist for a catalogue company. It was the best experience because I had to make cheap clothes look expensive and exaggerate the amount of fabric in clothes. My first role model was an artist in an ad agency. I was an apprentice-receptionist and was intrigued by a wonderfully talented woman whose work I loved. Apart from being talented, she was beautiful and fascinating with her continental accent, original style, and flaming red mane. I hoped one day to be like her, to have her flair. I would have loved to study with her, but we later lived on different continents.

A few more jobs, a few more years, and I moved on to a fashion ad agency in New York, which was the highest achievement for a fashion stylist other than in film. I had my own design clients and was the liaison between the client, the art director, and the photographer. My job was to cast fashion models for the photographer, get the clothes, accessories, and props for the ad, as well as hire hairstylists and makeup artists. There's a lot of sitting around between takes as the makeup artist and hairdressers retouch. I was on the set to make sure the garments fit correctly, no creases showed, and no detail was out of place.

The budgets in New York were big, the clients demanding, and the photographers tough perfectionists. Hundreds of thousands of dollars depended on a great advertising campaign that could make or break a label, so the pressure was to give clients plenty of variety and make sure they were happy. If not, they could take away their accounts and move to another agency. The perks were great; taxis were the only way to travel; the expense account was generous. And a private plane was available for a fashion shoot at an exotic location.

Everyone thinks that the models are magnificent, but you would not recognize some of them without makeup and with their hair in rollers. One model I worked with had a terrible squint and was able to focus just in time for the photographer to take a picture. Models are selected from a portfolio of photos. They do not necessarily have to be beautiful but they do need to have good bone structure. Usually models are very thin and tall. When choosing models, I looked for unusual shaped eyes, whether they are big and round, doe-eyed, or Eurasian looking. Some models know how to play up to the camera and can project different moods to reflect the atmosphere needed. They may not be particularly attractive, but they are very much at ease in front of a camera. A catwalk model is basically a thin clothes horse with good shoulders, the gait of a racehorse, and depending on the style of the moment, can be either plain, interesting, or have an attitude that stands out.

Working with top photographers was an eye opener when I saw the relationships they had with their models. Some were very rude, others helpful, but watching their skill in producing that fabulous, memorable ad was always exciting despite the bad temper tantrums of the art director or photographer.

I moved to London because I fell in love and married a man from England. Creativity leads you to different directions. I studied design and illustration in London and found myself concentrating on art. One of my exhibits, entitled The Moulin Rouge Collection, featured forty-five of my paintings and was unusual in that it combined three disciplines: fashion, art, and color. It had live models whom I dressed in the same style of clothing as the paintings. The effect caused gasps of surprise when viewers saw models dressed in costumes similar to those in the paintings. That exhibit was a lot of work, but it was well worth it.

One of my most exciting assignments as a stylist was selecting five models from around the world to represent

London, Paris, Milan, New York, and Tokyo. It was exhausting, as I also had to design the sets. It won an award, and I was really happy with the outcome.

I am still working as a stylist. At the moment, I have been commissioned to do a show for jewelers that combines art with jewelry—an exciting challenge.

Color is my thing. I love to coordinate color whether it's on a canvas, making a beautiful meal, or displaying it on the table. I love the visual arts, dance, and music. I enjoy ice-skating with my grandchildren. I also belong to a choir where we sing folk songs. I used to sing in harmony with my sister and miss her terribly since she passed away. Music can really heal the soul as can beautiful paintings. My greatest pleasure is to go to a wonderful exhibition at a gallery or museum. I love to work on ideas and projects, and when one excites me I can tackle it with such gusto that it absorbs me for weeks on end until I've exhausted it and myself. It could be painting or papier-mâché or writing or even reading. When I get into a book I usually finish it within a few hours.

I've lived my fantasies and look forward to doing exciting work in the future. I don't have any particular advice for others except to say that it's probably easier to persevere towards your goals the traditional way, one step at a time, starting as a junior and working your way up. I did it the unconventional way, but it doesn't always work out as we might expect.

My parents are my role models. I strive to emulate their values, love, and nurturing. I got encouragement and love from my sisters. Our mother taught us, "Money comes, money goes; the best insurance is a loving family."

My most gratifying success is my wonderful daughter who is really unbelievable. I am so proud of raising the most wonderful, creative, thoughtful, good, beautiful, generous human being.

My religion sustains me. I pray daily and observe my religious traditions. Religion gives me stability and adds a comfortable routine to my life. In times of sadness, it comforts me and puts things in perspective. But I tend to put myself in denial until I have to accept loss. Then I just sit and brace myself for the crash. Eventually I realize I just have to face it, get on with life, and look forward to the future instead of dwelling on the past.

For my epitaph I would like: "She was a good and honest person." I would like to be remembered as someone who added a little beauty and zest to living. I've enjoyed giving something substantial to my family and grandchildren, not money but perhaps an appreciation for good values, some skills, some fun and laughter, and instilling within them a love for family, life, and religion.

I feel so fortunate to have a sister who brings life, color, and excitement to my life, someone I can talk to and with whom I share family history. This conversation, which took place as a trans-Atlantic phone call, made me realize that time flies too quickly and I need to set a date to get together with her soon. Life has taught me, and is still teaching me, that we need to make time for the people we love.

YOUR THOUGHTS:

_____

_____

_____

_____

_____

_____

CELINA, THE PHOENIX

Celina is an activist who makes a difference in her community and at the same time develops herself as a person who grows with each new experience. She has known disaster, despair, and heartbreaking loss, yet they have made her stronger. She arises each time like the mythological Phoenix.

Celina radiates a quiet, inner confidence. She is soft-spoken, gracious, articulate. Her iron hands are encased in soft cashmere gloves and her vision is undeterred by the discouraging words of others—not an easy feat for a woman brought up to listen to powerful authority figures. She is a leader who has earned the respect of her peers.

I'm the youngest of six in a well-educated family. I grew up like a topsy. I did not have a lot of supervision, and I was very much on my own. I had the love and affection of my father, but my mother was difficult, distant, and preoccupied. I do not remember my childhood as being unhappy. l had five siblings and friends abounding. There was a lot of activity in the house.

I wasn't a good student in those early years, but I excelled in sports. I always had leadership ability but wasn't particularly aware of it. In high school I wanted to get into a top college. I was accepted and learned that I could succeed. That was a time of awakening for me as a young woman. The summer before college I met the man I married. It was a short courtship. We barely knew each other. It was a disastrous marriage.

While I always enjoyed learning and mastering a situation, the most motivating and truly important "push" was the sadness and trouble I experienced in my marriage. I felt that I turned myself inside out to please my husband, but nothing seemed to work. I really had nothing with my former husband, not to say anything about the actual circumstances of an emotionally abusive relationship.

I wanted something for myself, so I started building my life away from him. I became an activist for my own self-preservation. With this newfound conviction to grow beyond my problems, I discovered the pleasure and joy of going out into the world and doing things that made a difference.

I had just begun to develop my own identify distinct from my marriage when an even more devastating blow struck. In 1972, my youngest daughter developed osteogenic sarcoma (bone cancer) in her leg. After her amputation and subsequent rehabilitation with prosthesis, she was able to live only six months. She was an exceptionally vibrant child and adored by all who knew her. After I lost her, it took me a year to recover my emotional energy to take things on again, but I did, and with the conviction that I had to make something of the life I had to live.

I have a lot of spunk. One therapist told me I have a great ability: when I fall down, I brush myself off and go on again. I have an indomitable spirit. I didn't know I had those things in myself. It came with my experiences in life.

After my daughter died, I stayed in the marriage because I wanted to have another child, and I have no regrets. In addition to therapy, I kept busy with activities. I created a world for myself that had nothing to do with my husband or his social and financial powers. I found that I had an inner confidence and an innate creativity that others appreciated. I like undertaking a challenge and doing it the right way.

Eventually I did end the marriage. I showed myself and other women by my example, I suppose, that life does not fall apart when you leave your husband. My life expanded after I left my husband and became more involved in civic activities. Having some money helped because it enabled me to be out in the world. I could afford to go to a dinner at the museum. I could afford an event that was important to me because I was interested in the institution or organization.

I am a resourceful person who is able to build on experiences and actualize information into something appropriate to a new situation. Let me explain: Years ago, I organized a historical guiding service, the first to take corporate wives to historic Philadelphia. Later it became a popular service for private schools. When I returned to finish my undergraduate degree, I concentrated on art history and Philadelphia architecture. Then I created a walking tour of fashionable Rittenhouse Square entitled, "Philadelphia in the Age of Elegance." I was always intrigued with building one thing after another, as a child would. This seems to be a consistent pattern in what I've accomplished as an adult.

At the Philadelphia Museum of Art, I created an art appreciation course for seniors—an art and literature program focusing on creativity in later life that was presented to over 1,000 senior adults in the Delaware Valley. I wrote the script, planned the lectures, and trained guides who conducted the talks. I took the slide lectures to local libraries and worked on the program *pro bono* for five years.

I also founded and guided an endowment program for women within the Endowments Corporation for a Charitable Organization for 100 women, each of whom gave $2,500 to invest for future charitable gifts. It was a totally unique concept ten years ago when many women were not likely to think of themselves as philanthropists. But this program gave them the opportunity to take charge of a reasonable amount of money for their own charitable goals rather than just give to a yearly campaign run by others. Women of Vision, as this fund-raising project is named, has become a national model for other communities across the country. To date, we have 210 members and have raised over one million dollars.

In all the civic and cultural projects I've worked on, I have met with some adversity. It really takes a great deal of understanding and perseverance to accomplish things, and I am proud of my resilience in this respect. I think I have the ability to make things look easy, but they are not. I feel I've made a difference by setting an example for others because I have risen above the problems of a difficult, destructive marriage and the loss of a beloved daughter with dignity and achievement. I think people respect me for this and that is how I have become a person who deserves to be "listened to" when issues need to be ironed out. I am able to make good things happen. To me, this is very important.

People used to think I was just a "pretty face." I proved them wrong. I have discovered that I have good judgment, and if I can have the strength of my convictions, I will land in a good place. In difficult times, I do what has to be done.

The advice that stood me in good stead was "It isn't the money you have that is going to make you a happier person; it is what you can do for yourself." You can develop your mind. You can develop your body. You can develop yourself. You can work to feel physically fit—you can do that for yourself. And with a little attention, you can groom yourself and look nice. There's a lot we can do for ourselves.

These disciplined steps can give women a feeling of confidence. Creating our own lives gives us the strength to leave an unhappy marriage or an unhappy situation because, in the end, we are each left with ourselves.

Little things give me pleasure, like getting up in the morning and seeing the light outside, a gorgeous afternoon with the sun setting, or the cloud formations. I love the changing seasons. I love gardening. I'm a talented gardener and used to win prizes. I did not do it to win prizes; I did it because it was so much fun.

Fantasies? I once had a fantasy of being romantically involved and receiving great affection and kindness in a relationship. I am fortunate that for the past ten years, I have found a person who exemplifies some of these qualities and we are still together. I would like to be remembered with affection. And if I go to heaven, I would like God to say, "So nice to see you. Welcome."

What is that inextinguishable drive that enables someone to rise from the ashes? Perhaps it starts with an inner confidence—a tenacious confidence. That is what I noticed most about Celina. I found interesting the disciplined steps she lists towards building self-confidence: developing ourselves, working towards becoming physically fit, taking the extra few minutes to look nice, and working towards creating our own life. Sounds easy; I wonder it's as doable as it seems.

YOUR THOUGHTS:

_____

_____

_____

_____

_____

_____

HELEN, THE LIFE COACH

When I was a child I always wanted an older brother, someone who would listen to my problems and help me with homework or things I found difficult to handle myself. As adults, we can find people who can help us achieve our goals. Whether it is getting rid of clutter, working towards a new career, or putting our lives in order, the life coach is there to help. Helen is such a helper. I wondered how she became such a person . . .

Even as a little girl, growing up in a small town in Indiana, I knew what I wanted—to help people and make them happy. I dreamed of being a teacher or a nurse. My parents were sure that this is where my talents lay. I was a good student, and my parents were prepared to pay for my college education. What they did not expect was that I would fall wildly in love when I was fifteen and elope when I was seventeen.

My husband was my first boyfriend and my best friend, my knight in shining armor. It was no sacrifice for me to work in an office after high school and support George through college. We loved life, we loved being married, and money was not a problem because our parents helped us out. After five years of marriage, we decided that fun was fun, but we were ready for children. Two years later we had our first child, a lovely baby girl.

After her birth my husband changed. He was no longer interested in me sexually. He later told me it was because he didn't want to make love to "a mother." Still, we had another two children, twins, who were a delight. Yet our house was filled with anger and distrust. George had become more and more distant. We no longer laughed together. We had stopped liking each other. It didn't help that I had gained a lot of weight after the twins were born and couldn't motivate myself to take it off. Divorce was a tempting prospect, but the children were young, and I didn't have the qualifications for a good paying job.

My parents urged me to go to a marriage counselor and offered to pay for it. George refused to go with me at first, so I went alone. He eventually joined me at the therapist's office, and somehow we started to communicate on a different level. He had the courage to tell me how he felt, and I was able to understand him. It took time and work on both our parts, but eventually we arrived at a stage where we liked being with each other again. It wasn't easy. Yes, both sets of parents were supportive. Yes, we had a wonderful therapist, but there were times when both of us were ready to give up. Luckily George and I didn't want to give up at the same time, so we got through the rough spots.

I joined a weight loss program, my parents' treated us to the occasional weekend away from home while they babysat, and sex became fun again. I took time out for myself, met friends for lunch, and went for an occasional massage. This led to a renewed sense of myself. Gradually I was able to regain my self-esteem. Now, thirty-four years later, George and I have a solid marriage, and my husband is again my best friend.

He encouraged me to go back to school and become a therapist. I specialized in family therapy, which wasn't always gratifying because not every case had a happy ending. And it was painful for me to deal with unhappy children. After four years as a therapist, a friend who is a psychologist told me he was leaving his practice to become a life coach. The more he told me about coaching, the more it felt right for me, so I trained to become certified as a life management coach.

Unlike psychotherapy, which delves into patterns of the past and explores underlying conflicts, coaching is action-oriented. It concentrates on where you are today and how you can reach your goals. I love coaching and the variety of challenges it offers. I see clients who have trouble managing finances, salespeople seeking to improve their jobs, and women who are facing mid-life changes and need to clarify what they want to do. I don't delve into the past. The past is over and gone. My approach is "move on and I'm here to help you."

Most of my clients are receptive to doing "homework," and in some cases six weeks is enough to achieve a specific goal. A goal must fit these criteria: it must be specific, measurable, tangible, realistic, and controllable. A six-week goal consists of one action step per week. In weight loss, for example, the first week's action step may be eating in the kitchen only—not in front of the TV or elsewhere. Before taking these action steps, I discuss temptations and behavior habits with clients and we come up with alternative ways of coping. Some coaches do not meet their clients in person; instead they conduct thirty to forty-five-minute sessions over the phone. This is convenient for people who have a difficult time fitting an appointment into an already full schedule. Personally, I am more comfortable with eye-to-eye meetings.

Coaching has changed my life because I thoroughly enjoy what I am doing. I apply coaching techniques to my own goals, so I am becoming more and more successful in improving my own life. Sometimes I look back in wonder at the helpless, hopeless person I once was and am so proud of the confident, capable, and professional woman that I have become. Today I describe myself by the things I enjoy: I love life, I love my work. I enjoy celebrating with my husband. I enjoy fragrant perfumes. I like to laugh and have fun. I like to make people happy. I like to make myself happy.

I know now that nobody can make me unhappy without my help. I know now that I can help myself. I know now that I need to work on my marriage to make it work. I know now that life holds so much promise, even when I feel helpless and the future look hopeless. I look forward to working more, enjoying more.

If someone were to ask me for advice, I would say, "Let others help you. They may not give you everything you want, but it's better than nothing." During difficult times, my family sustains me. Organized religion does not play a role in my life, but I have explored spirituality, which I see as stripping away layers of toxins to reveal the light within.

I hope to live a long, full life, but when the time comes I would like my epitaph to read: "She helped others; she helped herself." I would like to be remembered as someone who helped make peoples' dreams come true. And if I go to heaven, I would like God to say, "Good job, Helen, good job."

How fortunate people are if they are able to find their passions in life. Passion seems to come so easily to the young. I wonder, can a life coach help adults find their passion in life?

YOUR THOUGHTS:

_____

_____

_____

_____

_____

_____

FLORENCE, THE OPTIMIST

I met Florence at a communications workshop that she was leading. I found her an interesting, innovative teacher. When we met again at the library and enjoyed a pleasant conversation, she described herself as an "optimist." I was curious to know more about what an optimist is. This is how she describes herself:

My friends call me an optimist. An optimist takes the same information as a pessimist and finds the good in it. But it's more of an intentional, conscious way of looking at things. My thinking is that, if you just give in to their way of "this is the best it's going to be," then you don't have a stake in improving the situation. An optimist invests in the future and looks forward to the outcome.

I always look forward to something. I believe happiness is based on recent good events—things happening now and things to anticipate in the near future. For example, if they are repairing the road and pulling up the pipes, people see it as a nuisance. I see that when it is finished, it will be a better road. Seeing the good is often seeing the bigger picture.

When I am invited to a party, I look forward to it for days. Sometimes if it's not a good party, my husband says, "See, you were so excited and it was not good." But my thinking is that I had the pleasure of anticipation. I had such a good time looking forward to it.

My husband is a pessimist, but he calls himself a realist. He calls me a dreamer. I see that his approach is not making him any happier. When he says, "You are a dreamer," he means it in a disparaging way, but I don't see "'dreamer' as a negative. I don't buy his interpretation. A lot of the things that realists told me to expect did not come to pass. For example, they told me that raising teen-agers was hard. This was not my experience.

Getting older has some downsides, but I accept them. The days of my being a size seven are long past, but now I no longer feel the need to jump on the scale every day. I always loved life. As a teen-ager, my philosophy could be summed up in Edna St. Vincent Millay's poem:

"My candle burns at both ends;
It will not last the night;
But, oh, my foes, and oh, my friends—
It gives a lovely light."

I used to dance all night long, get up in the morning, and do a full day's work. Now I don't dance all night long, but I still enjoy dancing. One of my dancing partners was a wonderful young man, full of life, energy, personality. He died suddenly, and I went to his funeral. The eulogy depicted a saint but did not reflect the man and who he was. I felt so sad. It was a lesson that changed my life. I asked myself, "What if they did that to me?" So I made up my own eulogy and whenever I feel like it, I write down the things I like. I keep adding to the list. I'm up to 119 and still going. And when I look back on what I have written, it gives me peace of mind.

Some of the things that I have written about: colors . . . , sequins . . . , coffee ice-cream . . . , letters from friends . . . , hot towels fresh from the dryer . . . , the feeling of satisfaction after a great meal . . . , the touch of my grandchild's cheek . . . , laughter—the laughter of my children . . . My family knows about this "eulogy" and knows where I keep it. When the time comes, as eventually it will, my eulogy will reflect the real ME.

In "the art of living," I live very well. I am happy that I am on good terms with everyone in my family, which is hard to do. I love my children and value them. I now have a new grandson, and I could never be unhappy because of this.

I think of friends as a garden, my human garden. I constantly weed my garden and allow new flowers, new friends, into my life. When necessary I reassess my relationships, and while I value the past and the good friends of my past, I don't feel obligated to carry them along into the future. If a friendship was good but it's not good now, I let it go. Maybe in the future it can resume, but for now it's over. Basically I get rid of the negatives in my life.

What do I do for pleasure? Everything I do is pleasant. When I must do chores I don't like, I do them to music. When I do paper work that I don't like, I play music that I love. So the music keeps me happy. I love to read. I love to write. I love to teach. I love to learn. I love popular culture. ("Wheel of Fortune," game shows. I don't like reality shows.) Having more money would give me the opportunity to be more generous, but when I don't have an abundance of money I still give of myself.

Life is ironic. When I was growing up, my mother urged me to become a teacher. I laughed at her! "Teaching, how utterly, utterly boring . . . tedious, uninteresting, ugh!" Now I am a teacher and see teaching as an almost holy connection between people. I just taught an adult education class in which we all wrote *Our Own Ten Commandments*. Some of the answers were fascinating. Two of mine were: "Think of how you want to be remembered and act accordingly," and "Don't whine unnecessarily."

The best advice I ever got came from my Dad. When I was in my thirties and wanted to go back to school, I asked him if he thought I should do it. He said, and I always remember his words, "Whatever you do, you will be a success." And he gave me the specific reasons he thought so.

Religion plays a role in my life. I love the holidays and the rituals that go with them. I appreciate the values of my religion and use them as guidelines. They work out very nicely. During difficult times, I am sustained by the awareness that life will not always be this way—that and my support system of family and friends. I don't believe in an afterlife, so if this is the only life we have, why not enjoy it to the fullest?

One of the advantages of getting older is that I have dropped a lot of the "shoulds" in my life, although I do admit that it would be nice to be more organized. The world is so rich and I savor it. I don't feel mature. I feel young. I don't have to hide who I am. There is a joy in me that keeps bubbling up. I can be myself. I can be an optimist. I can be spiritual. I can be silly and I can be deep. At this stage, I can be myself and if there are any consequences, I can accept them.

What do I want on my epitaph? "She was once a size seven." How I want to be remembered? As someone who made her immediate world brighter, more joyous, and funnier. If I eventually meet God, I would like Him to say to me: "You did your best."

I realized from this conversation that being an optimist is not as limiting as I thought it would be, that there is an awareness of reality. In her class, "On Writing Your Own Ten

Commandments," I was intrigued by her first commandment,
"Think of how you want to be remembered and act accordingly."
It's something I'd like to explore, perhaps with a friend.

YOUR THOUGHTS:

_____

_____

_____

_____

_____

_____

DIANE, THE CYNIC

Not all of us see life through rose-colored glasses. Diane is an attractive blonde who wears bright red lipstick and projects a glamorous image. She describes herself as "sixty-five living in a world of thirty-five-year-olds." She says that she feels thirty-five but accepts her biological age and enjoys the benefits of sixty-five years of life's experiences. A successful businesswoman, she describes herself as a cynic. How does she see life as a cynic and how does it affect her relationships with people?

I come from a family of six children. I have a twin brother. Mother was an invalid from the time I was four. I never had the privilege of seeing her walk. I was never able to have a mother in a true sense—someone who takes care of me, instead of my taking care of her.

I did not feel so deprived as a child, but in retrospect I realize it was a great loss. Yet because of my mother's condition, I am an extremely independent person. For years, I was a super caregiver. All the members of my family look to me for "salvation" to this day, even though I am the youngest.

My role model as a child was my aunt, my mother's sister. She dressed beautifully, wore vivid red lipstick, and traveled back and forth to New York on business. She was not particularly warm or friendly, but I thought she was an exciting, glamorous person, and I wanted to be just like her. I couldn't ignore the contrast, of course, between her and my mother in a wheel chair. I envied my aunt's daughter for having such a mother. Years later I learned that they did not have a good relationship.

Why do I describe myself as a cynic? I think I was a cynic even as a child. I saw other people's lives as fairy tales, not real—especially those people who were so happy. It couldn't be true or real, I thought. They had to be faking, putting on an act as if they were pretending to be "nice" for company, because reality was my life, what I lived with at home.

Being a cynic has affected every facet of my life. I very rarely believe other people. I'm very circumspect in my acceptance of other people's complimenting me or doing good deeds. I think it has to be for a good reason—it has to be for their own benefit—because they're expecting something from me in return.

A friend phoned to tell me she could not attend a meeting because she was very ill, in pain, and had trouble walking. I went to the meeting and there she was. I automatically thought that as long as she could walk, she must be fine. That is the measure of how I define illness. I learned to use this measurement because my mother was in a wheel chair for over thirty years—if you can walk, you're fine. I never accept my own illnesses. If I can get out of bed and walk, I'm not sick. Whether it's me or anyone else: if you are ambulatory, you are fine.

I don't go around being miserable or mean or suspicious of everything people say, but I don't get the full enjoyment of people's affection or even my own emotions. As an example, if I get particularly involved or happy in a relationship, it is always momentary. I don't place a proper value on it. I tell myself, "It's not such a big deal."

I don't know if this is part of cynicism or not, but I feel I have accomplished very little and should be much better—despite the fact that people in my business world tell me that I have accomplished quite a bit.

My relationships with my two married children and their spouses are excellent but I wonder how much of it has to do with my approach—"Zip open your purse and zip close your mouth." Even with my grandchildren, I come up with thoughts like, "They think I'm a bank." I don't know what would happen if I just stopped giving them gifts and only gave of myself or my time. What would happen if they could no longer depend on me for material gifts or money? If I do not hear from my grandchildren, my first reaction is, "When they call me, it will be because they need something." The inner question is, if push comes to shove, how much love will come through if I have nothing more to give?

In actuality, my children and grandchildren are devoted to me and love me as much as anyone else's children and grandchildren, but my cynicism remains with me because that question is always in my head. I don't allow myself to enjoy that love because l always question it.

I enjoy reading, especially biographies. I like sad books. I don't fantasize. When I was very young, my fantasy was that someone would fall madly in love with me because I was in love with love, as most young people are. The trials and tribulations of my life made me more cynical, and I had no more fantasies.

When my son was thirty and a practicing attorney, he was diagnosed as a paranoid schizophrenic. The child I knew had absolutely disappeared and was replaced by a stranger. It was my greatest loss. For someone to have had so much potential, to have this happen to him, made me even more cynical. At times the pain is almost unbearable.

It is not helped by the advice of my "optimistic" friends. I can't stand optimists and their platitudes . . . . "You'll see, he'll get better" . . . "God only gives you what you can take" . . . "Have faith" . . . When I think of optimists and their point of view, I think of this caricature of a 92-year-old optimist. "I always look on the bright side of life. I had two knees replaced, am fighting cataract surgery, can't hear too well, take twenty pills that make me dizzy and subject to blackouts, get mixed up between one way and two way streets, but my motto is 'If you believe it, you can do it,'—and nobody can convince me to stop driving."

Life has taught me an acceptance of what is. It's dangerous to delude yourself and it hurts to listen to advice when you are in pain. I never give advice to people. They don't want to hear it. You know what happened to Socrates when he went around giving good advice—they poisoned him—and I can understand why.

In difficult times, I'm sustained by the knowledge that I have the strength and ability to get through it as best I can. Religion does not play a role in my life. For my epitaph I only want my name—Diane. I would like to be remembered by my children as I am, a mother who always wanted them to be happy and was very concerned with their lives. As for meeting God in heaven, when I was a little girl I remember asking my mother if I would go to heaven if I were good. "When you're dead, you're dead," she replied. That made sense to me then and it makes sense to me now. I find it hard to understand that some people believe in life after death. But if there was a God, and I did get to meet him, I don't think I would speak to Him other than to reprimand Him for what He has allowed all of us to do to one another.

Life is certainly not a bowl of cherries for everyone. Who is to say that everyone has to be happy, that everyone has to see life as a joyous adventure? We are shaped by our parents and by our environment. We all do the best we can.

I've known Diane a long time. We are good acquaintances. We exchange pleasantries—how are you, nice seeing you, going on vacation? But we never really got to know one another until this conversation. I found it interesting that I felt closer to Diane after she trusted me enough to talk about her inner self. Maybe the lesson I needed to learn here is that being more open with another person can lead to a closer relationship.

YOUR THOUGHTS:

SISTER NELEH, THE NUN

When I was growing up in Canada, we lived in an area where French Canadians and immigrant families from around the world lived side by side in modest clean homes. Most quarters were on the second or third floors where access was via a winding, grilled, outdoor staircase. We lived next door to a large yard that was part of a convent. We used to watch nuns pace back and forth in groups of eight or ten as they recited their prayers. We were mesmerized by the shiny beads and crucifixes they fondled.

Five minutes from my home near Philadelphia is another convent. When I pass by, I sometimes wonder what it's like to be a nun today. And that is why I interviewed Sister Neleh, a tall woman dressed in a slacks suit, with a pleasant smile and easy laugh. I wanted to learn what she thought about the art of living.

When I was in a Catholic grade school, I went to Mass every day. At that time, I knew just what I wanted to do: I would love to be an FBI agent. I would love to be a writer. I would also enjoy being a detective. In this life, I have done all three in the service of the Lord and His people.

As a teacher, I needed to be a detective, and I had to be able to write and express myself. Most students are honest, but some cheat. They copy magazine articles and pass them off as their own. I didn't want to give an A+ to a cheat, so my detective abilities came in handy. I also did handwriting analysis—and I can tell liars by their handwriting. When I analyzed handwriting, people liked it. I would say things like "You are interested in the sciences" or "You are too generous for your own good." I was usually on target. I like people and sometimes I could help them that way.

Before I entered the convent, nobody expected me to be a nun. Even when I first came to the convent, some of the other sisters asked me, "Why are you here?" I'm sure some of them are still thinking that because my problem in life is that I tell people what I think—and sometimes they chuckle. It's not what people expect me to think and say. I feel that there isn't a set way you have to think and, because I am a nun, I don't have sound holier than thou or "nunny."

Last year two elderly volunteers told me that they had tickets for a bus ride to a casino in Atlantic City, but they'd missed the bus. I told them not to be upset. I was not working on Monday and would drive them to whatever casino they wanted to visit. I thought it might be fun. It would make them happy, so why not? I wagered ten dollars and, while some people would be shocked, I don't see any harm in doing that. Besides, I am giving the elderly ladies the pleasure of an afternoon off.

When I entered the convent, I expected to have a quiet life away from the world and to be obedient, like the stereotyped saints you read about. Instead I found that nuns are just human beings struggling with life just like everybody else. We don't have husbands and children to worry about. We do have many people whom we deal with and are concerned about, so our vision is a little wider than the average family person who's primarily concerned about the immediate family.

When I first came here to the convent, I looked around at all those different faces and wondered who was nice and who I did not want to be with. I found out that we were all the same. We all had the same goals. We were on the same journey to God and the only way to go is by helping people along the way and by living and teaching as Jesus did.

When young women first come to the convent they are called postulants, which means a trial period where they are seeking, searching, to learn if God is calling them to this religious life. When they receive the veil and the habit, they are called novices. Again, they are still seeking, trying things out. The first novice year (called the canonical year) is much stricter than the second year because the older nuns want to see if the novice belongs, and the novice too wants to find out if it is right for her. It is a two-way street.

As a young nun, I was energetic and had a nimble mind that kept me busy. The first time I was allowed to work outside the convent, they sent me to a psychiatric hospital to help priests who had problems. Many were nervous or disturbed. I worked with them, tried to get them to relax, and played cards with them. Then Mother Superior sent me to fill in for a sick nun who was a Latin teacher. That was a happy experience for me because it was something I could do. I enjoyed doing it and felt appreciated.

After I took my vows, I was assigned to teach a third grade. I was so used to working with adults that when I got these third grade students, I used to kneel down and pray, "Dear God, help me to like teaching them." This was the life I had chosen. I had vowed to be obedient, and these third graders were a challenge. So I prayed every night. By Thanksgiving, I had gotten to like them. I felt great about it. That was my first experience in teaching children. Each year I taught a higher grade of elementary school, then high school. In the interim I had earned a degree in math so I taught it in college.

Some students lived on campus. Many of their parents were in the military and moved often, so they sent their children to board here. Some did not like being away from their parents, but we tried to make a nice home for them. There was one young student who had an uncontrollable temper. One day he lost his temper with me and I lost mine. I slapped him and told him that he should not have talked that way. Then I said to him, "I lost my temper and you lost your temper. We are both guilty." We talked. I listened to what he had to say, and he seemed to comprehend what I was saying.

Thirty years later we had a reunion. He told me that that incident had changed his whole life. He had always wanted to be a basketball coach and was able to get the job he wanted. But he lost his temper, stopped coaching, and went for counseling. He never coached again because he was afraid he would lose his temper. Instead he became a counselor for the basketball team. He had remembered what I had told him, and it had made a difference in his life. He named his first son after my father.

I'm now seventy-eight and have been in the convent for sixty years. I spent the last thirty-two years teaching at a catholic college. Most of the students were in an international group of Muslims, Buddhists, and a couple of Catholics. They come from abroad and reside here for their college education. We teach English as a second language. We prepare them to go on to other universities. Some stay on and decide to work here, to help others. When I retired, the person who took my place was a young Japanese woman who married an Ethiopian man who also came to learn English. In fact, we have twelve couples from other countries who met here and got married.

Now that I'm retired, a typical day for me is less strenuous. I go to Mass at 6:30 A.M., followed by prayer. I then make my bed, tidy up, and like most of us, I go to work. My ministry is working with outpatients at the hospital. I don't wear a habit so most people don't know I'm a nun.

One of the good things about being a nun is that I have more time for the Lord. The whole reason for coming here is to get in touch with the Lord or to have Him get in touch with us. I say "He," but God has no gender.

What I tell students who have had hard lives is, "God did not promise that everything would go well. He just said he would be with us." And that is very comforting. No matter what, God is with us and He will be with us.

Prayer is being with the Lord, being aware that there is a Lord, and God is everywhere and He is with us. Prayer is not only praying to God; it also is listening to Him. That is why a retreat is so important, to have time away from the hubbub. That is why the Lord gave us the Sabbath, a day for the Lord.

Religious orders have three vows: poverty, chastity, and obedience. There is another one that we call the fourth vow—service to the poor and the sick, which includes teaching the ignorant or the uneducated.

We can feel lonely if we don't have children of our own or someone who loves us. That is a sacrifice we make for the Lord. I think we are all searching for God, but some people do not know it. There is dissatisfaction in all of us because we want things to be permanent and remain the same, and nothing does. The only one that remains the same is God. He loves us no matter what we have done or who we are. God loves us. The only real commandment that God really gave us was "Love one another as I love you." Sometimes that is hard for me, and I say a prayer for forgiveness.

I have time for leisure. I like to read, play cards, listen to music, walk, garden, and arrange furniture. I look forward to being even more aware of the Lord in my life. When I was at a retreat last week, we were disturbed by a few interruptions. A priest said something that stayed with me:

"When we are interrupted, when we are doing something that we think is very important, we see it as a negative. But actually God is in the interruption." Or as St. Augustine said, "God writes straight with crooked lines."

During difficult times I am sustained by knowing that God is with me. My motto is: "God's will be done." I have no special words I want for my epitaph—except perhaps, "She tried." I would like to be remembered as a loving person. And when God greets me, I would like to hear Him say, "Welcome home."

So much to think about after this interview . . . Praying to God includes listening . . . God is in the interruptions of life. I remember reading something about the interruptions in life being what life is all about. It's an intriguing concept. When I go for a walk this afternoon, I'm going to reflect on what Sister Neleh said.

YOUR THOUGHTS:

_____

_____

_____

_____

_____

_____

MARGUERITE, THE PHYSICIAN

I was suffering from a sciatica nerve pain for two days when a friend suggested that I see her osteopathic physician, Marguerite. My friend mentioned how "marvelous" she was, particularly for her age—ninety-two. I was curious how a woman could function well at that age, let alone elicit good results from her patients. I thought that if I could learn how this doctor maintains her mental agility and physical dexterity at ninety-two, perhaps I would learn something that would help me when I got older. So I interviewed Marguerite, and this is what she said:

When I was five years old, I was run over by an automobile and taken to an osteopathic hospital. I was in a cast for four months. After I left the hospital, I had a great deal of sciatic nerve pain and was treated by an osteopathic physician who normalized my pelvis and helped me get back to normal. He became my family doctor, and I became convinced of the power of osteopathy.

I never missed a day of elementary school, high school, or college. I attribute my good health to his osteopathic manipulations, so when it came to selecting my profession, I naturally wanted to be an osteopathic physician. I have been lecturing for thirty-five years on osteopathic manipulation and anatomy to students at an osteopathic hospital. I teach standard medical subjects, concentrating on anatomy. I also tell them that if they want to get appreciation, "handle a patient not like a machine, but as a human being."

Because students know if I am not prepared for the lecture, I need to take time to study and keep up to date. This keeps me on my toes. A few years ago, when I was barely able to walk because I was healing from a fractured rib, I overheard a student say, "Oh, man, this old lady isn't going to teach me anything! She can barely move." By the end of that year, I had the satisfaction of having him tell me, "Your knowledge is amazing, and I really learned a lot from your class."

I can name every muscle and bone in the body; I can adjust all twenty-six bones in the foot with six manipulations in ninety seconds. But I cannot operate a microwave oven!

I not only correct and mobilize the structures in their bodies, but my patients know I really care for their welfare. I try to follow the golden rule, "Treat the patient as you yourself would like to be treated." It may sound trite and old-fashioned, but it works for me, and it's what I teach my students. In addition to teaching, I have my own practice for seventy years, and I have no intention of retiring. What I love most about my work are my patients. They have become almost like family, especially those I have been treating for three to four generations. One seventeen-year-old patient said to me, "Don't die—don't ever die—my grandmother needs you, my mother needs you, and my generation and my children need you."

Three years ago I fell at home on Easter Sunday and fractured my rib. I was back in my office nine days later. I could barely walk, but I was able to see six patients a day and help them. It took me a while to get to the treatment table, but when I was there I could do what I needed to do. As an osteopath, I believe if you can align the body, nature herself will heal the body. A few months ago I fell and fractured my wrist. The surgeon asked me how many times a day I was exercising my fingers. "Incessantly", I answered, and that has helped in the healing.

I was honored two years ago by township commissioners for "extraordinary dedication to her patients and her profession of healing." I found it rather ironic, because sixty-eight years ago they called osteopathy "witch medicine." I received other awards, but the one I appreciate most was being named, at the age of ninety-one, as "Teacher of the Year" by the Pennsylvania Osteopathic Family Physicians Society, which also gave me the Frederick J. Solomon DO Award of Merit.

I am fortunate that that we have longevity in my family. My grandmother was in her seventies when she died; an aunt lived to be ninety-five and an uncle was ninety-six when he passed away. But I do believe that my having osteopathic manipulation has kept me in good shape.

I am very fortunate that I have a wonderful husband who helps me. He does all my accounting, pays the bills, and fills out the insurance forms—things I don't enjoy doing. He was an accountant and it's second nature for him. In addition, he cooks and drives me to work.

If I were to give one bit of advice to women, I'd say "Marry a man younger than you so he will be able to take care of you." My husband is seventy-five. We have a very happy marriage. We have been married forty-three years. I had been married before. My first husband died of a heart attack. Four years after his death, I met David. He came into my life as a patient. He was in terrible pain and I was able to alleviate his misery. He kept coming back for little things, until finally I said, "David, you're in better shape then I am." He replied," If you don't think I'm too forward, I would like to ask you out for dinner." I made sure I looked nice, wore my lacy blouse and high heels, and made myself as attractive as I could because I knew this was a man that I wanted.

To quote the old cliché, life includes both the good and the bad. For me, these are good: I love my work. I read a great deal. I like adventure and travel stories. I enjoy the respect of my colleagues. I am proud that I have thirteen letters after my name, all of which I earned through conducting research, teaching, and publishing papers.

The bad: For a long time I enjoyed swimming, but I had to give that up. I loved traveling; now I travel only to conventions. As the years go by, it takes more effort to do things that used to be easy. I had a malignant polyp removed from my colon and underwent chemotherapy. I have my bad days when I don't feel well or walk well, but that does not stop me from doing my work.

I had three children with my first husband. Two of my children, both smokers, died of lung cancer. It is sad and heartbreaking, but I am grateful that I still have one child left. My patients keep me going, with remarks like, "Now, doctor, I know you're having a tough time, but I'm in pain and I need you."

I have a great deal of faith. I have been a member of my church for eighty years. That carries me along. My husband is a great companion and joins me in church activities. Basically, I would say that faith and the church sustain me in my most difficult moments. Because of my religion, I have spiritual help: I realize I don't carry the heavy load alone. That has carried me along all the years of my life.

When I die I want my treatment table to be buried with me—in case St. Peter has sciatica. I want my epitaph to read: "She helped, comforted, and eased the pain of her patients and friends." I would like to be remembered as one who cared for everyone she came into contact with. As to what God might say to me, it would be nice to hear,

"You lived a good life and helped a good many people in the course of your life."

Talking with Marguerite reinforced my belief, that we all need a reason to get out of bed in the morning—something that gives us pleasure, something we enjoy, or something that helps others. When my mother was ninety and wanted to sleep most of the day, the aroma of coffee enticed her out of bed. It might be interesting to list what it would take to get me out of bed in the morning, when I am older, and on a day I was not feeling well.

YOUR THOUGHTS:

_____

_____

_____

_____

_____

_____

AGATHA, THE SOCIAL WORKER

I somehow believed that social workers have a better way of dealing with life than most people because they have the experience of helping others deal with difficult situations. I wondered if my assumption was true and decided to interview a clinical social worker. Agatha, a tall, attractive blonde with big brown eyes and a gentle, non-intrusive way about her, spoke freely about her experiences as a social worker.

When I was entering the job market in the late 1940s and early 1950s, there were not really too many things for a woman to do. She could be a teacher, nurse, secretary, librarian, or social worker. I tried the secretarial route, but that was not for me. After I left my secretarial job in a hospital, the head of the social services called and asked me if I would like to work for her. That seemed better than what I had been doing, so I started working for her. I think my technical title was "case aide" because I did not have a Masters degree. I worked at the hospital for a couple of years and, as I look back, I think I grew a little bored because I did not see myself as developing. There was no teaching connected to the job that would help me advance. So I resigned and went to Europe. I had a few dollars saved, so why not? When I came back, I thought I would try something different. I got a real estate license but did not enjoy being a real estate agent. It took a huge amount of time. My time was not my time: my time became the buyer's time, so I became a case aide again—this time at a children's agency in the foster home department. In this position, I was instructed and not left on my own.

Then it dawned on me that there was a vast body of knowledge to learn. So after working there a while, I enrolled in the Bryn Mawr School of Social Work where I had a very good experience. There was individual attention, and I caught on to the fact that I had better get hold of a lot of knowledge—and I'll tell you something, it never stopped. There's always more to learn. That is why the field is so darn interesting to me.

When I started out, I was very naïve about social work. I had no idea how rich it could be. Most of the work gave me a feeling of satisfaction because social workers are always helping people, and there are different levels of help. It could be very superficial or very profound, like having clients change their way of dealing with life. No matter if it's the most superficial or the other end of the spectrum, it's rewarding.

It's also satisfying to figure it out. You can figure out what the problems are at many different levels so there are a lot of opportunities for satisfaction. My work has taught me a lot about life, but most of all it encouraged me to learn about myself. I think it is less true today in schools of social work and in practice, but as I was developing one was always challenged with questions about how one's own personal feelings were shaping your work. Letting personal feelings and attitudes influence your work was not in the best interest of the client, and my generation was constantly challenged to examine what was inside us. If we were aware of what is going on within ourselves, attitudinally, that awareness could certainly shape relationships and communication, which may not have always been in the client's best interest.

During their most difficult moments, clients can get themselves up in the morning if they have a core of optimism. This enables them to cope, in my experience. Optimism is not always available to them, but sometimes they had access to a relationship in which there was optimism. That core of optimism really has its roots in early infancy. Infants need to have someone on whom they can rely to calm them, who can comfort them so that they grow up with a sense that things can be better. In my opinion, the core of the therapeutic relationship—if the therapy works—is that the client can find calm in the relationship.

What advice would I give to others? "Don't give advice." I think people pretty much have their own solution to their problems. I am not a very good advice taker, but the best advice someone gave me as a child—not that I knew it was advice then—stood me in good stead. It will make you laugh: "Behave yourself." I don't always do it, but I try to and I think it has helped me in life.

I tend to be introspective. I think I'm very hard on myself, and I monitor my behavior a lot. I play back in my mind what I've said and done, and I wonder whether it was the best thing to do. Maybe being a social worker and wanting to do the best possible job has something to do with it. On the other hand I like to have fun, and I'm funny so I guess it balances out. And I enjoy life—I enjoy almost everything I do.

I have fantasies of all sizes—but I don't like to talk about them. I will say that as a child I dreamt of being a schoolteacher. I probably would have been a good one. But I have no regrets—I loved being a clinical social worker and still have a small private practice.

My husband and I had a very happy marriage. We had no children, which perhaps made us made us self-indulgent in that we just had to take care of one another and enjoyed doing that. I met John when I was a social worker at a children's hospital and he was a resident physician and in child psychiatry. People sometimes asked me what it was like being married to a psychiatrist. My answer was simple: It's no different from being married to any nice person.

My husband died four months ago. The support of my friends sustains me in difficult times. Religion plays no role in my life. For my epitaph I would like: "She was terrific." I would like to be remembered as a nice person. And if God were to speak with me, I would like Him to say, "Come on in. All your friends are here and they are planning a party."

Four months after the husband she loved died, Agatha was able to go on with her life, see clients, and accept the comfort of friends. How was she able to do it? Perhaps one answer lies in what Agatha said about her clients: "Some people have within them a core of optimism." I think those words apply to Agatha herself.

YOUR THOUGHTS:

_____

_____

_____

_____

_____

_____

JULIETTE, THE CARING CLOWN

Juliette is my mentor. I worked with her for years as a volunteer clown at a children's hospital, and I admire her tremendously. No matter what the weather or how she feels, she's always there with her red nose and silly clown outfit to entertain sick children with magic tricks, puppets, and stories. Here's how she talks about her work and herself.

Volunteering as a clown is my passion. I could not do anything else. I feel something guided my footsteps toward doing the work I do. I just know I have to do it. It's work and it's fun. It's exhausting but invigorating at the same time.

I have different clown personalities. Usually I'm Dr. Sovta with an array of toy medical tools. Another personality is Jeppy, named after my daughter's imaginary friend whom she played with when she was a little girl. When I told my daughter I was going to be Jeppy, she had a far away look in her eyes. And then, of course, there is Shnips. That was the name that my husband used to call his big sister when he was a little boy. It annoyed her terribly, which is why he did it. When I told him that I was going to use the Shnips personality, he had the strangest look on his face. I guess it made him recall what happened when he was a kid. He could not believe that I had remembered that name.

Most of the time it's fairly easy to make children laugh, to diffuse anxiety for both children and parents. But there are always the difficult cases. One incident stands out in my mind: I saw a little boy, held in his mother's lap as a nurse tried to put a shunt in his arm in preparation for medication. It took two parents, an uncle, and several members of the staff to hold him still. He was terrified and screaming. I went over to them, blew bubbles, and tried various stunts to distract him. The little boy kept screaming, "Don't do this to me. I don't want to die." That stopped me dead in my tracks. I turned away so he could not see the tears on my cheeks. As I walked down the hospital corridor, I felt a hand on my shoulder and a gentle voice saying, "It happens to all of us at least once."

I took a deep breath, turned to my fellow clown, and said, "We've got a job to do. Come with me." It took the two of us to calm him down and eventually get him to laugh. The staff and parents were very grateful and waved a cheery goodbye as we went on to the other wards.

Being a clown gives me the opportunity to meet wonderful people. Many are driven by something inside of them, a "knowing" that they must do this clowning, this teaching, this mentoring, this entertaining. At clown conferences I meet circus people, teachers, sales people, and magicians. Some sell various kinds of equipment, but they will not sell it to you unless you demonstrate, in front of them, that you know how to use it. No matter how awkward you feel trying out a new stunt, you can't be self conscious with them. "Practice, practice, practice when you get home," they tell you encouragingly, "and the next time I see you, show me that 'shtick' again." They really care. It's amazing.

Clowns have opportunities to visit different countries, like China, Japan, Africa, and Russia. Patch Adams, the maverick doctor who does clowning, feels people have a need to laugh.

When he takes groups of clowns to different countries, they bring their therapeutic humor to orphanages, hospices, and schools for the blind. They communicate through the universal language of love, laughter, and compassion. One of these days I'm going to go on one of his tours.

Working as a clown taught me the importance of laughter. Experiencing life taught me to accept what is. Life isn't perfect but who expects it to be perfect? During the tough times I tell myself, "This too shall pass." I do the best I can with what I have. I have gone through some terrible times. I got out of it stronger and learned something along the way.

As a way of relieving tension, I belong to a laughter club. Yes, I'm serious. A laughter club. Every once in a while we meet for lunch at each other's house and laugh, just laugh. No jokes, no funny stories. Someone starts the ball rolling with a "Ready . . . One, two, three—chuckle; four, five, six—chortle. Come on, you can do it . . ." and then gives a hearty "Ha-ha-ha and a ho-ho-ho-ho," and before you know it even the most humor-impaired start to laugh. It's contagious. After five or ten minutes of laughing, we end up weak with laughter and ready for lunch. While laughter may not be the best medicine, I agree with Oscar Wilde that, "Life is too important to be taken seriously," and while I'm laughing, I'm not thinking of my aches and pains.

Like everyone else, if I can't solve my problems, I live with them as best I can. When people ask me for advice, I try not to be a know-it-all. What works for me doesn't necessarily work for others. People have to think their way through their own problems, but some just need a little push. My motto is: "Don't sweat the small stuff," but you really can't teach that to others.

Life has so much to offer: I love many things: reading; having my husband rub my feet while we watch TV; getting up early in the morning and enjoying the quiet with a cup of coffee; talking to people in the supermarket. People like to talk, and I like to listen. I ask them what they do, and that starts them off. Some people are lonely and welcome a chance to talk about themselves.

Sometimes I have this fantasy that I'm traveling all over the world, and in every country I visit I speak the language fluently. The reality is that I have a lot to look forward to, including a painless old age, I hope. I have a supportive husband who helps me through the difficult times. We talk things through. We don't always agree, but that's okay.

Religion plays a role in my life. I believe God put us here on earth and gave us brains so that we can figure out what we should do. I don't know if there is a heaven or a hell. I think we make our own heaven or hell here on earth. I have a personal relationship with God. On Friday night when I light the candles, we talk. He or She does not always answer me, but then again I have all my relatives to tell me what to do.

When I die, I want my funeral to be fun. I don't want my family to cry. I want them to remember the laughter, the fun. I want a service where everyone celebrates, not mourns. The most wonderful funeral that I ever attended was for a much-loved Shriner clown. The lobby of the church was decorated with his clown costume, stilts, big clown shoes, and photographs from his clown life. And the minister honored him by wearing a red nose.

For my epitaph, I would like: "She had a sense of humor or she could not have raised seven children without killing herself, or them." I would like to be remembered as someone who enjoyed laughter and people.

I had forgotten that incredible feeling when you do it "just right" and see the relief in the eyes of the parents and hear the laughter of the children. The recollection makes me smile for days afterwards. I haven't clowned since my mother died. I've been meaning to go but . . . .

YOUR THOUGHTS:

_____

_____

_____

_____

_____

_____

SONIA, THE WIDOW

Ten years ago, a friend who lost her husband told me how important it was to be "prepared for widowhood," and sent me a list of all the things I needed to discuss with my husband immediately. I felt sick! In no way was I prepared to face this possibility. And even if I were, how could I go to him and say, "Darling, when you are dead and buried, I need to know that I will be financially secure?" I tore up the list—I knew my husband could be trusted to take care of these matters. Since then too many of my friends have discovered that "ignorance is not bliss," and I have since made sure that I know what to do should something happen to him.

My dear friend Sonia's husband Jim died a year ago. Whenever they sent a card, they always ended with, "Together always, Sonia and Jim." She was his true love, and he voiced his appreciation almost every day. They had no children. She devoted all her energy into making life easier for her husband. They were always together. They worked together. Neither had a hobby or interest that they did not share with one another. They were a lovely couple who could truly be described as "soul mates." It was impossible to imagine how one could live without the other. But life sometime makes the unthinkable a reality and the question is, how does one bear the pain? Let's hear from Sonia to see how she was able to survive.

Nothing was as painful as my husband's death. In the beginning, everything was completely blank. My mind did not work at all. Not at all. Rest and rest and rest, but I was always tired. Then I was kept busy. The papers started to arrive. I got the death certificate. I had to straighten out all the accounts, and I did not know how. It was so frustrating. I spent hours on the phone, asking various people how to get the necessary documents, how to fill them out, where to send them. Attending to all these things cost me a lot of nerves and took a lot of energy.

As much as I was hurt by Jim not being with me, I was blessed because I had wonderful neighbors who came by every day to cheer me up. I had to get dressed in the morning because I never knew when they would show up. My next door neighbor comes to visit often because she wants her children to have a substitute grandmother. She lost her mother when she was very young, and it's nice for her to come in, talk a bit, and know that her children are appreciated. I always have some cookies for her children and a few small gifts to make them happy. Every four weeks they make a "family dinner," and I am included in their family.

I have another neighbor who lost her husband and needs me. I try to help her because my neighbors, complete strangers, helped me. I never really talked to the neighbors in my apartment building and never expected that they would ever take an interest in me. My husband and I had made some friends, and every Saturday and Sunday they take me to the park and we have dinner out.

Another elderly couple also came and helped me. When the husband got sick, I felt I had to do something to help them. When he was in a wheelchair, I wheeled him to the park. When he got better, I convinced him to walk more. Now he says, "Let's go!" He's walking every day. He and his wife invite me to dinner sometimes.

I started working once a week at a Catholic Charities senior center where I serve food to the patients. They need my help and asked me if I can give more time. I am now going to work twice a week.

I begin my morning early and go for a walk around 8:00 A.M. When I come home, I'm hungry and tired. Then I do the little things that have to be done in the house. In the afternoon I go for another walk and somehow the day is done. I play bridge once or twice a week, and in the evening I read. I don't watch much television except for the news.

I try to live as best I can with what life hands me. I like the lack of obligation. When I want to get up, I get up. When I want to go out, I go out. I walk for hours by myself. That is when I am most happy.

After my husband died many neighbors who were widows told me about their frustration after their husbands' had passed away. Well-meaning friends tried to comfort them but only made them feel worse. When the widows wanted to talk about their pain, the comforter started talking about a similar situation in her own life or someone else's life, which is the last thing the recent widow wanted to hear. Or they said, "Everything will be okay," which was not what she needed to hear, and that put an end to any meaningful conversation. The worst sayings were those like "God would not give you something you cannot bear." The only comfort really was a sincere "I'm really sorry" or a hug from a friend.

They were totally unprepared for the many things that had to be attended to and which caused confusion and a feeling of helplessness. One widow made out a list, "What every wife should know," that she gives to anyone who asks for it. This is how it reads:

- Once a year talk with your husband about the state of your finances and what he recommends you do if something happen to him. (Examples: distribution of possessions, whether to sell the house, and what you need to do).

- Do you know where the important papers are? (Insurance policies, health insurance documents, titles to cars, old tax returns, deed to house, will and living will).
- Do you know where the safe deposit box is? Are you an authorized signer for it? Do you have the key?
  It is important that you know your husband's Social Security number. You will need it.
- What is the cash flow for your lifestyle? What is in joint names? What is in your name? What would you do for cash for the first month?
- Do you have your own checking account and credit card?
- Who is your lawyer? Accountant?
- If your husband was in business, know where the ownership papers are; if there are partners, know which percentage of the business is owned by whom. You will need a lawyer to deal with the partners.
- Do you or your spouse or parent have a family owned business? What will happen if they die?
- Obtain a death certificate (in triplicate, as you will need a few original copies) as soon as possible. You will need it for the bank if you want to change the account from two names to one. Another death certificate has to be sent to Social Security immediately so that the amount can be readjusted for the spouse. There is also a certain amount of money that Social Security pays towards funeral expenses.

Have you discussed funeral wishes? Do you know where you own cemetery ground? Do you have a copy of your address book handy? If something happens when you are away, others can make telephone calls for you.

When things get back to normal, check your credit rating twice a year, with all three of the credit reporting agencies. You might not need credit, but it's a good way to find out if someone has managed to use your credit cards without your knowing it. DON'T MAKE ANY MAJOR DECISIONS FOR SIX MONTHS TO A YEAR.

She ended it with: "Should the unexpected happen, you must be prepared."

When friends suffered a loss, I tried to comfort them by saying things like, "At least he didn't suffer" or "This too shall pass." Until Sonia mentioned it, I hadn't realized how painful this approach was to a person who had suffered a serious loss and wanted to talk about the loss but couldn't because these words cut off lines of communication. It's not that I wasn't sensitive to their suffering; I just wanted them to feel better. It hurt to see them unhappy, and I thought those words would be of comfort.

YOUR THOUGHTS:

_____

_____

_____

_____

_____

_____

OREA, THE SOLDIER'S WIFE

Military life is foreign to me. I sometimes wonder how a soldier's wife adapts to having to move repeatedly to different cities, different countries, leave friends, make new ones. When I met Orea, I had the opportunity to learn more about the quality of adaptability:

I never had any desire to visit the USA, but here I am living in Cherry Hill, New Jersey. After my military service in Israel, I worked for three years as a secretary in Tel Aviv. In 1962, I went to Paris with a girl friend and stayed for six months while I studied French and worked at the Israeli Embassy. I had lots of friends, traveled to Europe occasionally, and basically had a good time.

Life is ironic. You never know where it will lead you, especially if you marry a soldier. I was living in Israel with my father, a widower, when I met my husband Ray. His cousin wrote us that Ray was coming on a visit to Israel and asked if we would show him around. At that time not everyone had a car, so my father was asked to do the job because had one.

When we met, Ray was a captain in the United States Air Force on leave after spending two years in Viet Nam. During his stay we fell in love, but Ray had to go back to Viet Nam. We corresponded for a year. Then he came back to Israel and we were married. After the wedding, we moved to North Carolina where Ray was stationed.

Not only did I move to a country foreign to me in many ways, but also to the South, which is an adjustment by itself. I knew English quite well when I came to the U.S, but it was hard to understand the southern accent, even for Ray. Over the years, people used to ask me where my accent was from, and I jokingly replied "Texas." Some people believed me.

I could not get used to the "officers wives syndrome" that was a big part of military life in the 1970s. The wives' club, the little ladies with hats and gloves and afternoon tea gatherings, were not my style. I tried to stay away as much as I could. I had to attend some of the functions because Ray was a squadron commander and it was expected of me. I guess I was not a "good military wife" and was very glad when we were transferred to Italy, where this role was not necessary.

After three wonderful years in Italy, where our first daughter was born, we came back to the U.S. and lived on a military base in New Jersey. Fortunately, Ray was sent back for another tour of duty in Italy. We stayed in Italy for another four years and our second daughter was born there. We had lots of Italian friends and were happy to be back in Italy. The Italians are very wonderful people, kind and accepting. We made good friends, and to this day we still keep in touch.

Ray had five remote tours before we got married, two in Korea, two in Vietnam, and one in Labrador. But we were lucky that during our marriage Ray did not have to go on remote tours, meaning remote places where soldiers cannot take their families.

I liked moving from place to place, seeing new places, and meeting new people. The hard thing was leaving friends behind, especially in Italy. I had to develop a mechanism to block my emotions on the day we left. Otherwise I think I would have fallen apart every time. The friends we made in the military are our friends for life. We stay in touch constantly, and even though they are all over the U.S., we manage to see each other occasionally. The wonderful thing about the military is that your religion is your private affair. It belongs in your home and in your synagogue or church, and people are treated as people, not according to their religious affiliation. Wherever we were stationed, we had a Jewish chaplain or a lay leader. In Italy, I was teaching Hebrew school to five Jewish military kids.

When Ray retired as a lieutenant colonel, we decided to settle in Cherry Hill, New Jersey, so I could live closer to my sister. For us, remaining in one place at that stage of our life was good. Ray got a job with the ROTC in a nearby town. We made new friends, and we love the area we live in.

For our girls, who were born to us later in life, the move was not difficult. Usually military children move around until they finish high school. Ray retired when Nora was in fifth grade and Talia was in kindergarten, so they did not have to go through the trauma of changing schools and leaving friends behind. They graduated from high school in Cherry Hill and formed friendships that they did not have to leave behind. They often tell us how fortunate they felt in that respect.

There are advantages to growing older, one of which is that you learn how to better adapt to life. From years of adapting through military life, I learned three basic things: To take a deep breath before answering when angry (though it doesn't always work!); things eventually work out for the best; and being happy comes from within because no outside forces will make you happy if you don't have it within you.

And what I would tell others is: Make every day count. I learned that at a very early age. My mother died at the age of thirty-eight when my sister was eight and I was twelve.

The only positive thing that came out of this tragedy is that I don't take any day for granted.

Life has so much to offer: I enjoy cooking, (because it is very creative and relaxing); being involved in volunteer work; traveling to new places; and occasionally meeting a friend for lunch or going to the movies. I also enjoy these "small pleasures:" the first cup of coffee in the morning; a nap in the afternoon; a movie or a play that remains with me for days; a good book; conversations with my daughters; hugging my granddaughter; having people for dinner; home and my animals; small portions of delicious food in a good restaurant; and dreaming. I have a whole world that I live through my dreams, sometimes wonderful and sometime upsetting. I remember most of them and usually can connect them to split-second thoughts that I had during the day.

Each morning I try to accomplish my trio of activities: Exercising (for the body); praying (for the soul); and solving the cryptogram in the newspaper (for the brain). When I accomplish all three, it makes me happy, but some days not all get done . . . . But life is not perfect.

On a less happy note, ten years ago Ray developed scleroderma, a life threatening illness that affects different organs: skin, lungs, and liver. Sickness changes everything. Ray's illness was and is the most difficult issue I've had to deal with in my adult life. After a couple of years of dealing with Ray's scleroderma, I had to be helped by an anti-depression drug that I am still taking. The fact that Ray has been doing relatively well for the past ten years helps me to go on. Faith and support from my sister, who is my best friend and soul-mate, has helped me during the most difficult times. She is my support when I need a shoulder to lean on. I look forward to growing older with Ray in good health and enjoying our family, and I hope we can do more traveling.

Religion plays a role in my life, but not in the conventional ways. I find direct connection with God without the mediation of a rabbi. For me, my place of worship is in my heart and at home. I do pray every day in the privacy of my living room. We keep the tradition of the holidays and the Sabbath. And to my joy, our girls do, too.

I would like my epitaph to read, "She loved life." I would like to be remembered as a woman who tried her best in everything she did. If God spoke to me, I would like him to say, "You can go back now . . . ."

What I found particularly interesting were the advantages Orea saw in growing older and the things she enjoyed in life. I read so many books, but somehow I learn more from what people like Orea tell me.

YOUR THOUGHTS:

_____

_____

_____

_____

_____

_____

HARRIET, THE WARRIOR

I had my annual mammogram two months ago. During the three-day wait until I received the written report that I was okay, my thoughts dwelt on what would happen if the diagnosis was bad. What would happen to my husband? How would he manage? The children? My grandchildren? How would I cope?

While waiting for the result, a friend told me that her smart, full-of-life mother had a very malignant form of cancer and was told she had only a 10 percent chance to live. Harriet was given the choice to accept radical experimental treatment or to let nature take its course. After much thought and long discussions with her husband, she decided to opt for the experimental treatment. Here is Harriet's story as my friend, her daughter Wendy, tells it. It answers many of the questions I asked myself and shows us many different ways we have of taking control and coping.

Diagnosis confirmed—My mom has breast cancer. Okay, now what? She gets chemo, right, and everything is okay. At least that is what everyone keeps telling me. I don't know how to feel, except it hurts really badly inside. Every conversation with my mom seems to bring even worse news, but she is her usual upbeat and strong self. Why doesn't she cry? My mom is a registered nurse and understands a lot of medical jargon. She is facing a very aggressive form of breast cancer that has affected seventeen out of twenty of her lymph nodes. Without aggressive chemotherapy, her survival rate is low. But what does aggressive chemo and radiation mean? And even with this, there are no guarantees except that she will be very ill and will lose her hair. My mom is a woman who can handle anything as long as she is in control.

When she began exploring her treatment options, it wasn't without a lot of input. My sister, the oldest of my siblings, can gather more information and research than anyone I have ever met. She is also great at voicing her thoughts and opinions, regardless of whether you asked for them. My sister informed us that Mom was the one who had to make the decisions.

As Mom put it, "I want to be in my own home, my own bed, and throw up in my own bathroom." This was hard for us to hear because we wanted her to get the best treatment wherever that may be. This was the first lesson we learned: Mom needed to be the one to determine her course of treatment. My mom took the initiative and contacted her nephew at Duke Hospital who set up a second opinion. That doctor confirmed the nightmare but agreed Mom could get all the treatment she needed at her local hospital.

So thirty days after surgery, the first round of chemo began. We were all with her when the horrible side effects began. She was sick and exhausted. We all agreed the person whom we needed to worry about was our dad. Again, my older sister came through with a great book for a husband to read when his wife has breast cancer. It hurt to see the strongest man in the world look lost and scared. It broke my heart. My dad and brothers shaved their heads to show support. Mom responded, "Wouldn't it be funny if I don't lose my hair." My nieces and nephews thought their dads looked scary. My mom has thirteen grandchildren. Each seemed to handle the news differently. They all sent weekly pictures, letters, and gifts to inspire their Granny, as she was not permitted to see them until after her chemo was completed.

She lost her hair as she expected and accepted this like a real trooper. She never once mentioned her baldness in a negative light. She shopped for wigs and scarves and cracks us all up with the new shopaholic she has become. Mom showed us our second lesson: You need to accept what you cannot control.

My mom became really ill with an infection that the doctors had a hard time fighting. The antibiotics didn't seem to work and the chemo was delayed. Mom received a digital camera and agreed to send us photos. Much to my amazement, I opened one of the photos and it was a picture of her infected breast. I almost died. I called her, and we laughed at the thought of my husband's expression had he been the one to open the picture. This was when we gained our third lesson: Always keep your sense of humor.

The lack of control seemed to set in when she found herself in the hospital once again. She doubted her treatment. The doctor reminded her, "In this journey we never look back." WOW! How true that you cannot second-guess your decisions. I totally got why she didn't want to be in a hospital. Have you ever tried to get some sleep? Not to mention, trying to get out of bed without exposing yourself? When she was in the hospital, she always put on one of her hats (that look like ski hats) and walked the halls. When she ran into people, she would laugh and ask if they had seen her skis. This made everyone so much more at ease.

She was released and found herself admitted again, this time with pneumonia. She hit rock bottom when one of the nurses sat with her and asked to pray with her. The timing was perfect, and she realized what she can and cannot control.

Our family is very religious and relies strongly on our faith during this time. Our faith has helped the grandchildren understand, as they all know God is watching over Granny. Surrounded by friends who jump over each other to help, Mom sees and values the need to receive instead of to give. Boy what a role reversal! She sees the need to receive for my dad as much as for herself. Another valuable lesson: Create a support network.

My mother doesn't want to suffer and has made her wishes known via a living will, as well as a last will and testament. Though I pray every day that we never have to take this route, my family is clear about what she wants if her treatment plan is not successful. Our final lesson: Establish provisions in case things do not proceed as planned.

Where do we stand now? We wait for what is best. Mom is fighting hard and undergoing her first round of chemo. When that is finished, we will get a better picture of where we stand. No matter what the results are, we have learned a lot and know that Mom will make the best choice. We pray that she is with us for a really long time, but only if it is a quality of life that she chooses.

When we get really bad news, what is the first thing that most of us usually do? I know that I start thinking about "what if's." They usually are not all that positive, and I find myself feeling really down and waiting for the next bombshell. Well, that wasn't the case with my mom. When the rest of us were trying to stop crying, she never lost her sense of humor and play. I heard the saying, "A day without laughter, isn't a day worth living."

That is definitely the motto my mom has displayed. She was able to find the humor in many of the "insensitive" comments that so many of us make when we stumble over which words to say to someone going through a tough time.

Given the choice of crying or laughing, she always finds the humor in almost everything.

What an incredible woman; what a supportive family! I learned that I don't have to let a situation control me. I can choose to take control. I can decide on treatment options and how to deal with them. I don't have to do it by myself. I can reach out to family and friends for a support system and make sure that my wishes are carried out.

YOUR THOUGHTS:

_____

_____

_____

_____

_____

_____

VIVIAN, THE VENTOR

I learned about "venting events" from my friend Vivian. A group of participants get together to vent their issues in a non-confrontational way. The goal is to reduce stress. The idea behind these group events is that people who keep things to themselves, who do not share with their friends or relatives, carry an unnecessary burden. Talking out problems in a safe environment can be therapeutic and leave the individual feeling much better.

When things become overwhelming, Vivian sometimes hosts a venting event. I knew she had been going through a particularly rough time with both her husband and her aging parents, so I was surprised when Vivian called to invite me to a women-only party the following Sunday afternoon. She lives in a large Victorian house, a little neglected, but quaint and charming.

I arrived a little late. Vivian ushered me into the living room with twelve women I'd never met. A coffee table held a box of tissues and a few platters of Melba toast and low-fat cheeses. Vivian asked each of us to stand, introduce ourselves by first name only, and mention our favorite dessert. I was Anne—Apple Cake. I found this part fun. After we had nibbled at the food, Vivian told us why she had invited us.

"I'm having a hard time in my life right now, and misery loves company. So I thought we would all let our hair down and talk a bit about the things that get us down in our lives. I chose to invite you because I trust you enough to confide in you and know you would never repeat the confidences shared in this room. There is only one rule: No advice. We are here to share and to listen. Who wants to start?"

Dead silence.

Vivian looked at me, "Anne, why don't you start?" I stood. The eyes of twelve strangers were upon me. Vivian gave me an encouraging smile. I shot her a desperate, pleading look. "You seem upset," said Vivian sweetly. "Won't you share with us what is troubling you?" I bit my lip and took a long, deep breath. Then I thought, what the heck, why not start the ball rolling?

"I *am* upset. Last week I rejoined my weight loss group. This time I was *absolutely determined* to lose ten pounds. I asked the group motivator why their food plan never works for me. 'Because you don't want to work at it, and you don't follow the food plan,' she said. I felt sick! I knew she was right. I don't want to write down every morsel of food I eat, I don't want to deprive myself. I don't want to do what it takes. Who am I fooling? I'm never going to lose weight. I'm never going to be able to button my skirts." I felt my voice rising as I repeated, "Never! Never!"

"I wish I had your problem," interrupted Bertha—Banana Cream Pie. "I'm fat, fifty, and need to lose at least forty pounds. I went shopping last week. Looked in the full length mirror and . . . . "

Lucy—Lemon Meringue Pie spoke next: 'I decided to have liposuction and it's scheduled for next week. It's the right decision for me. I tried everything else, but now every time I open a magazine I see articles about the things that can go wrong and even if it's usually safe, what if something goes wrong? And . . ."

"Fat is not what I wanted to be when I grew up," stated Dorothy—Chocolate Chip Cookies. "When I was married, I wore a size eight dress and now when I step on the scale . . . . "

"STOP IT! THERE MUST BE MORE TO LIFE THAN LOSING WEIGHT. I DON'T WANT TO HEAR ANOTHER WORD ABOUT FAT," shouted a voice from the back of the room.

There was a long silence. We all apparently agreed.

A new voice spoke up. "My marriage is breaking up. My husband is the most wonderful man in the world and I love him, but I have a mother-in-law from hell. She never liked me from day one. She talks against me all the time. He hates me because I'm not nice to his mother, and I hate him because he listens when she talks against me. I don't know if my marriage can survive the constant fights we have because of her."

"I can understand that," said Michelle—Chocolate Ice Cream. "Mothers-in-law can be wrong, but nothing is more heartbreaking than a daughter-in-law who won't let you see your grandchildren. My daughter-in-law is a vegan, and that's okay with me. But her children don't have to suffer because of that. They always look pale and undernourished. I read an article that too much soy is bad and sent it to my daughter-in-law. She ignored it. Last time my grandchildren were at my home, I was so sorry for the poor dears that I gave them their first decent meal—some chicken, rice, and a nice plate of blueberry pie with ice cream. They told their mother. She phoned my husband, told him that she will never allow them to visit us again, and she does not want to talk to me. The worst part of it is that my husband blames me. I tried phoning her to apologize but . . . ."

Sarah—Homemade Strudel interrupted, "You're lucky you have a daughter-in-law. My son just met a young blonde, and now he's living with her. She hates me and won't let me talk with him. When I call in the morning, she says he's sleeping. If I call during dinner, she says he's eating. I call at ll:00 P.M., and she says he's busy. Busy! What could he be busy doing at eleven at night that's more important than talking to his own mother?"

"I can relate. My son never calls," added another voice. "The last time he phoned, I didn't even recognize his voice. When I told him that, he said if that's the way I'm going to talk to him, he won't call again and banged down the receiver. Now I don't know whether to call him and apologize or wait for him to call and apologize."

The woman next to her nodded sympathetically. "Ungrateful children are a curse from God. I'm a single mother and sacrificed everything for my son and daughter. I could have married and had an easy life, but I didn't want my children to have a stepfather. Now my son lives in California, and I never see him. My daughter married rich and doesn't want to know me. This year they didn't even send me a birthday card."

"I know how you feel," another woman added. "I don't ask for much. I never did. All I ever wanted is a little appreciation. I've been married for thirty years, and I don't think I once heard my husband say 'Thank You.' All l want to hear is 'Thank you' just once before I die. 'Thank you.'

"I don't need a thank you," said another woman, "All l want is a little understanding, just a little understanding . . ."

An attractive woman in a smart pinstriped suit said in a low voice, "I left my husband after seven years of marriage. He never understood me. I felt life was too short to waste on a marriage that was meaningless. We had no children. I had a great job. I didn't need his money. I wanted to explore life while I was still young. I hoped I would meet someone who could fulfill me. It's been one year since I left him, and I'm scared. It's a tough world out there, and I don't know if I have what it takes to make it. I'm so frightened, but I don't want to go crawling back . . . to what?"

When she had finished, Vivian stood and said, "I applaud you all for your courage in sharing. I know it's not necessary, but I want to repeat that everything said in this room is confidential. Now I'm going to ask you to bear with me."

She then proceeded to give a fifteen minute impassioned monologue that made King Lear's life look blissful. Vivian told us that her mother has Alzheimer's disease, her father has had two auto accidents and refuses to stop driving, and her retired husband is depressed and taking it out on her. Vivian was squeezed between her parents' and her husband's problems.

At the conclusion of her story, with tears streaming from her eyes, she looked upwards, raised her hands imploringly, and cried, "GOD! WHAT DID I DO TO DESERVE THIS? WHY ARE YOU PUNISHING ME?" At that she stopped, wiped her eyes, blew her nose, and said, "Thank you. I feel ever so much better now."

No one said a word. No one moved.

Vivian started to apologize for taking so much time and being so dramatic. But before she could finish, we all stood up and gave her a tremendous round of applause.

Vivian beamed. "Thank you, thank you. And now, before you go, for those who want to indulge I have some little goodies that I prepared for you." She ushered us into her dining room where the table was laden with chocolate chip cookies, brownies, lemon meringue pie, gobs of ice-cream, and Vivian's specialty, a five layer chocolate mousse.

"Help yourself," said Vivian. We all looked at each other. Vivian had obviously spent many hours preparing this feast. How could we insult her by not taking any dessert? So we each took a plate. I decided to have just a little taste, and another little taste, and another . . .

When we left, we all felt happier and lighter. Well, not exactly lighter . . . but there are times when one simply can't count calories. "A wonderful afternoon," said Emily—Linzertorte. "The best ever!" echoed Sarah—Homemade Strudel. "We simply must do this again," trilled Susan—Sponge Cake. An absolutely splendid time was had by all, and we agreed we should do this more often.

When Vivian invited me to this event, I didn't know what to expect. I was uncomfortable at first, but as I look back with a humorous eye, I'm so glad I attended. We shared laughter, tears, compassion, and understanding. The experience showed me that listening to other women's stories—especially without rendering judgment, as Vivian instructed us at the outset—puts our own problems in perspective. A venting event isn't for everyone, but if you decide to attend one, I offer a gentle reminder: Don't wear mascara.

YOUR THOUGHTS:

RAE, THE ADVOCATE

My family came to Canada from Czechoslovakia. During World War II, our entire family in Europe was killed, with one exception. I was only a child, but I still remember my father's face when he received letters from his brothers, "Save us, save us. Get us into Canada." It was not possible. To be alive and to live in a free country were privileges that he could not give to his family. To this day I have a special feeling for those who make it possible for others to live in a free country. Let us see how Rae, an advocate in an immigration agency, sees herself and her role as an advocate for those in need of a safer, better life.

An advocate sees injustice or unfairness in the world, either in a particular situation or on a more general level, and works to make a difference. That could be either by working on a one-to-one basis with an individual who has been treated unfairly or by bringing public attention to a situation. As an advocate in the immigration area, I am involved with helping people become Americans and maintain the unity of their family.

Last week, after working with a client for three years, the exhausting work finally paid off. She was granted permanent residence in the United States. All her children and grandchildren were citizens. At that moment, she broke down in tears, kissed me, and kissed the immigration officer. She told us that she had not seen her father for twenty years. He was ill with cancer, but she had not been able to visit him because if she had left the United States, she would not have been able to reenter. Now she can travel to the Dominican Republic to see her father before he dies.

During those three years as we worked together to try to get her papers, she had experienced many moments of despair, but she was a survivor. She was in a very abusive relationship with a man who threatened her with a knife. To escape, she once jumped out of a window, broke forty bones, and had seven operations from the injuries. But she survived and now has her green card. She can apply for U.S. citizenship in five years. I told her that if I'm around, I would help her apply for it.

For many immigrants or refugees, making the difficult journey to America is a journey of survival and hope. My mother came from a small village in Poland, where her family were dairy farmers. She often went to bed hungry and afraid that she and other family members would be assaulted or worse because they were Jews. The level of stress and anxiety that my mother and her family faced was extremely high. Even so, it takes courage to leave behind your country and community. It is hard to imagine all the things an immigrant must learn to start a new life in the United States. When my grandfather came from Poland, he had never seen a banana before. He thought the peel was the fruit and the inside was the seed. So he ate the peel, of course!

I got into this field because I am the daughter of immigrants. I grew up in a community where everyone was first or second generation Americans. I went to college to become a social worker and got my Masters in social work. Several years later I went to law school with the goal of becoming a poverty lawyer—a lawyer for people with low incomes. From there, I landed here, helping immigrants.

Both my parents influenced me. My mother was an immigrant from Poland. She was only able to have two years of formal education, but she was very smart. She was a garment worker who became a union organizer. She was always concerned about the welfare of her co-workers and the community. My father was very different. He went to Yale on a scholarship when he was fifteen. He was an idealist and a humanitarian. They raised me to value relationships, intellectual achievement, and creativity. We didn't have much money, but we had a very rich, fulfilling life.

I'm a bit of a workaholic but I enjoy my family. I enjoy cooking for holidays, reading novels, hiking, and canoeing. I try to keep physically fit and belong to a fitness club. I try to go four times a week but don't usually make it that often. I enjoy spending time with friends, going to movies with them.

I look to the future: I look forward to the birth of my first grandchild and I look forward to going to work every day. I work very hard, and in a few years I look forward to working less. In the future, I hope that immigrants will gain more acceptance. Immigrants built America, and they still should be valued and respected.

When I retire there are a lot of things I would like to do: take classes, learn another language, do pottery. I'd love to act. I used to act in college. That is one of the things I like about my job. I like the litigation part: It gives me a chance to use my public speaking skills.

My fantasy is to have a summer home, perhaps on Cape Cod, some place very gentle, near an ocean. A place that's pristine, not overdeveloped.

Now that I am older, I am more tolerant of human frailties. I realize that part of being human is making mistakes. What I have not learned is how to say "no" when somebody asks me for help, but I'm getting better at it.

If I were to give advice to others, it would be: Remember what's important in life. Contribute to people or to your community. It doesn't have to be a big thing. Be honest. Try not to be selfish.

I didn't get much advice from my parents. Instead, I got role models. One of the things I recognized about my mother was that she had made tremendous sacrifices so that I could get an education. She had to work long hours, but when she came home she was a wonderful nurturer. Having my own children and raising them was the most meaningful part of my life, but it took a lot of juggling because I was working full time.

I identify as being Jewish, belong to a synagogue, and celebrate the holidays, but I am not a traditional believer. I reflect a lot on the belief that there is something larger than us out there and that we can draw upon this for strength. My family and my values sustain me. After I survive a painful situation, like the sudden death of my father, I become stronger. The wisdom that comes from experience helps put things into perspective.

For my epitaph I want these words: advocate and humanitarian, wife and mother. I want to be remembered as an advocate who made a life long commitment to fight poverty and prejudice. If there is a heaven, I would like God to tell me that He will take care of the people I left behind.

I appreciate and respect people who devote their lives to helping others. Rae's face shows signs of fatigue from working long days. She could work shorter hours and make much more money in different areas of law, but she chose this route. As a daughter of immigrants, I am grateful that there are people like her. Every generation has different role models. I wonder who the role models are for my grandchildren. I think I'll ask them. It should lead to a more interesting answer than the "How was school?" question.

YOUR THOUGHTS:

BARBARA, THE CAREGIVER

I first met Barbara at a yoga class. When we went out for lunch after class, she talked about her life before she was married and some of the courses she had taken over the years. She told me about meeting a professor at a party and falling in love with him. The next day she called him and said, "I'm giving a party on Saturday night. Could you please come at 7:30?" He arrived and saw the table set for eight people. She invited him into the living room where they sat down and talked. About nine o'clock he looked at his watch and asked, "Where is everybody?" She gave him a big smile and with a gleam in her eyes, said, "I only invited you!" This is not an unusual story in today's times, but this took place in the early 1950s when women did not do that sort of thing.

I lost touch with Barbara after the classes ended, but I bumped into her twenty years later. The years had taken their toll, but that spark was still in her eyes. Again we spent time over lunch. This time she told me the story of her life as a caregiver:

I met Ralph when I was eighteen. I was young, romantic, and idealistic. He was handsome, wealthy, and showered me with presents. He told me that he had diabetes and did not expect to live more then twenty years, if that. If I married him, he later told me, his life would be filled with happiness. I believed him. I had visions of going on cruises, wrapping a blanket around him as he relaxed on a deckchair, making sure that there was no draft, spending my life making him happy.

It didn't work out that way. Most of the trips we made were to doctors. The only money he gave me was for the household expenses, and the only happiness I gave him was when I catered to his every whim. Ralph had no interests. He was totally preoccupied with himself and his health. He always complained and expected constant service from me.

Friends who came to visit told me what a wonderful husband I had. (He never complained to others and could be charming when he wanted to be.) Friends mentioned how lucky I was to have him and what a lovely home I had. I don't want to tell you how that made me feel. And I couldn't say anything. One didn't air one's dirty laundry in public in those days, so how can I tell friends about an angry, miserly husband and how that has affected my life? I was miserable. He was miserable. We were miserable.

People have told me that God only gives us what we can handle. I was too much of a lady to tell them what I thought of this saying. Then something happened that changed me. I attended a class where the guest speaker was a renowned psychologist. He told us that the first question he asks a patient is "What's good in your life?" For one hour he lectured on the importance of realizing the positives in one's life. That talk made me think about what was good in *my* life. I realized that there is always a positive side and a negative side and each moment *I* can choose one or the other. I decided I want the positive side, and that is how I try to live my life.

I have music. I have books. Even though most of my friends have moved to Florida and new friends don't have the same flavor, I still have good friends. I take classes, and once a year I go to a spa. Ralph understood that if he wanted a caregiver, he had to let me take care of myself.

Sometimes I have regrets. I wish I had listened more to the stories my father told me about life in Russia. My mother told me that when they were going to America in a horse and wagon, her grandmother ran after them crying, "My child! my child! I will never see you again." Father was a cobbler's apprentice. He wanted to tell me stories about his life, but I did not want to hear them because they were too sad. He did mention that at night he read by candlelight and slept on the bench where he worked making shoes.

I have some other regrets: I wish I had finished college. I wish I had left my parents' home and learned more about life before I was married. I wish I had been more adventurous. I wish I'd had sex before marriage. I could go on and on, but the only really painful regret is that I did not adopt children. That still hurts.

Sometimes I have the fantasy that I had a grateful, appreciative husband and am surrounded by happy, smiling children and grandchildren. Then that old pain comes up, but I remind myself what self-pity did to Ralph, and I don't let myself dwell on it. Basically I have a good life. I enjoy and look forward to many things. I embroider, listen to classical music, and take interesting courses.

I should mention that my husband became diabetic when he was only twelve. Can you imagine going to birthday parties and not being able to eat the cake or ice cream? His family kept it a secret that he was a diabetic. In a child's mind when there is a secret it is something to feel guilty about. Ralph never really accepted being a diabetic. Once when we were on a long plane trip, he did not eat lunch, which caused him to become hypoglycemic and brought on reactions similar to being drunk. He needed food at this point. Experience taught me that as time goes by, the severity increases. I had to find food and force-feed him.

Can you imagine me—on a plane, with strangers looking on—trying to put raisins in his mouth while he's slapping my hand? This did not help, so I asked the stewardess for some jam, and we both tried to force it into his mouth. In the 1950s a diabetic would be sent to the hospital to regulate his sugar. A nurse told me once that it took three orderlies to hold Ralph down so they could give him an injection of glucose. Fortunately a pump was developed that helped me enormously. The pump is set so that little spurts of insulin are injected periodically during twenty-four hours. When a diabetic eats, the pump adds more insulin according to what was in his meal.

Dealing with a sick and difficult husband often filled me with anger, which upset me even more and made me feel guilty. So I took courses in stress and anger management. I have a bad temper, and when Ralph used to call me for the tenth time, to get him this or give him that, I thought I would explode. Deep breathing exercises and yoga helped. But this anger management technique worked best: When things got bad, I would go to another room, take out a plump pillow, a tennis racket, and proceed to beat that pillow until I was exhausted. Then I wiped my eyes, went to the kitchen where I had a nice, hot cup of tea with a slice of chocolate cake, and listened to music. I felt drained, but in control.

I also took a three-day course on journal writing that changed my approach. It brought up many insights, many very deep thoughts. After one class, I went to a nearby restaurant. When a waitress came over to take my order, I asked for a cup of coffee and a sandwich, served together at the same time. Two minutes later she came and plunked a cup of coffee on the table. I felt a rage coming up from my stomach. I could feel my face flush. She hadn't listened to me! What incompetence! Then I realized—more than anything I learned in the whole class—that a small thing like that could upset me. The interesting thing about this was that I never would have noticed if I had not been writing in my journal. Now when I feel myself reacting the old way, I can change my thinking. I do deep breathing and hum to myself to change my focus.

Life can still be fun. I taught myself graphology (handwriting analysis). I once gave a party and asked each couple to bring another couple whom we did not know. I asked the new couples to write me a hand-written note, not typewritten, written with a pen, not a pencil. I then analyzed their handwriting from their letters. At the party, after we ate, I told everybody what they were like, based on their handwriting. It was the most fun. Every woman called me the next day to tell me what a wonderful time they had and said I was right on about their husbands. The husbands did not call.

If I had to give one bit of advice to women, this is what I would tell them: "Don't believe everything your husband tells you." If you ask your husband before a big party if you need to go to the hairdresser, and he says, "Your hair looks perfect just the way it is," don't believe him. If he assures you that you will be well taken care of when he dies, assume he means it, but check it out. You could be in for a very unpleasant surprise.

Ralph lost most of his money in the stock market, and we had to sell our lovely home. I still have enough money for my basic needs. I can live with that. My motto is: "Count your blessings, not your problems."

Ralph died two years ago. I wish I could say that he thanked me before he died for all the years I took care of him. He didn't. Pain and illness made him even nastier. But it didn't matter so much. I felt very sorry for him. He had lived his illness instead of living his life, and I still managed to live a life of my own in spite of his illness.

What would I want written on my epitaph? "She was not a martyr."

I admire Barbara. Being a caregiver year after year is not easy. In the process, one's own needs are often ignored. I like her statement about Ralph's living his illness and her living her life. I have a tendency to let another's sick bed take over my life. I need to remember Barbara's example if I'm ever in that situation again.

YOUR THOUGHTS:

_____

_____

_____

_____

_____

_____

MARION, THE CARING NURSE

When my mother spent some time at a geriatric ward of a Montreal hospital, she was one of the lucky ones. She had family who visited daily and stayed long hours by her bedside. Many patients had no visitors. It was my impression that, because my mother was obviously valued by her family (and perhaps because someone was always at her side to ask for help when needed), the nurses gave her more attention than others. It was a busy ward. The hospital was understaffed, and the nurses could not meet the needs of all the elderly patients. Most nurses performed their duties in an efficient manner, but few seemed caring or gentle. Marion, however, stood out in particular for her compassion. Somehow she reached out to every patient; she seemed to see them as human beings, not old bodies taking up space. She always made time to say a few reassuring words, sometimes staying with a patient and holding their hand. I asked her, "What can children do to get better care for their parents? Gifts, cash, even pleading doesn't seem to help. What would you do if your mother was in the hospital and you were not able to be with her?"

Writing a note to thank a nurse when she's been particularly helpful would be nice, and it's sometimes put on the wall. I can't speak for the other nurses, but I would bring pictures of my mother when she was younger and put them on the wall in her room, or maybe include some drawings from great-grandchildren. This might help the nurses, who are usually well meaning but overtired, to see my mother as a person not as a very old woman.

When I first worked in the geriatric ward, I found it difficult because I'm a visual person and very old people are not attractive. It was very hard for me. I mentioned this to the head nurse and told her I wanted to work in another ward. The head nurse listened, and then gave me a poem that I keep in my purse and look at whenever I feel myself beginning to become numb.

The poem apparently came from an old lady in Scotland who was in a nursing home. When she died, someone went through her things and found a poem she had written. Some nurses made copies of the poem, and it was later published in the magazine of a mental health association. This is the poem:

> What do you see, nurses, what do you see?
> What are you thinking when you're looking at me?
> A crabby old woman, not very wise,
> Uncertain of habit, with faraway eyes?
> Who dribbles her food and makes no reply
> When you say in a loud voice, "I do wish you'd try!"
>
> Who seems not to notice the things that you do,
> And forever is losing a stocking or shoe . . .
> Who, resisting or not, lets you do as you will,
> With bathing and feeding, the long day to fill . . .
> Is that what you're thinking? Is that what you see?
> Then open your eyes, nurse: you're not looking at me.
>
> I'll tell you who I am as I sit here so still,
> As I do at your bidding, as I eat at your will.
> I'm a small child of ten . . . with a father and mother,
> Brothers and sisters, who love one another.,
> A young girl of sixteen, with wings on her feet,
> Dreaming that soon now a lover she'll meet.

A bride soon at twenty . . . my heart gives a leap,
Remembering the vows that I promised to keep.
At twenty five now, I have young of my own,
Who need me to guide and a secure happy home.
A woman of thirty, my young now grown fast,
Bound to each other with ties that should last.

At forty, my young sons have grown and are gone,
But my man's beside me to see I don't mourn.
At fifty once more, babies play round my knee,
Again we know children, my loved one and me.
Dark days are upon me, my husband is dead;
I look at the future, I shudder with dread.

For my young are all rearing young of their own,
And I think of the years and the love that I've known
I'm now an old woman . . . and nature is cruel;
'Tis jest to make old age look like a fool.
The body it crumbles, grace and vigor depart,
There is now a stone where I once had a heart.

But inside this old carcass a young girl still dwells,
And now and again my battered heart swells.
I remember the joys, I remember the pain,
And I'm loving and living life over again.
I think of the years . . . all too few, gone too fast,
And accept the stark fact that nothing can last.

So open your eyes, nurses, open and see
Not a crabby old woman; look closer . . . see ME!

I read the poem and found it extremely painful. I could not reread it for a long time. But somehow it changed me in a way. After my mother died, I found myself volunteering at the geriatric ward of the hospital. At first I tried to communicate with the patients, but it didn't work. Then I learned to say just a few reassuring words, gently hold their trembling hands, close my eyes, and imagine that I was holding my mother's hand, that I was doing this for her. Somehow it felt good.

YOUR THOUGHTS:

_____

_____

_____

_____

_____

_____

_____

MILLIE, THE MATCHMAKER

I met Millie at a dinner party. A charming, likeable woman, she entertained us with stories about people she met when she was a social coordinator in charge of activities aboard a cruise ship. We talked about loneliness, and we agreed that loneliness is one of the biggest problems in our society. It came as no surprise, therefore, that Millie's favorite hobby is matchmaking. She discusses her life and her experience as a matchmaker:

People need people. People keep me young, keep me interested and interesting. I get a lot of pleasure introducing people to one another, "making matches." Many times my children teased me and sang the song from *Fiddler on the Roof*, "Matchmaker, matchmaker, make me a match, catch me a catch . . ."

It's a challenge for me to arrange dates for people who are older, who have not dated for a long time. Most of the women are uncomfortable, nervous, and afraid of not making a good impression. Some are too anxious. If I feel they are receptive to advice, this is what I suggest on a first date: There's no need to be nervous. All you have to do is to be yourself. Just pretend you are going out with a friend. I would let the other person introduce a topic. This way, you get to know what interests him. If it is relevant, you might ask "If you had to do it all over again, would you still have done it the same way?" Be observant. Look for something nice to say. If you notice something you like about him, mention it . . . . nice voice, nice eyes, whatever.

If you read the newspaper the day before, you have something at your fingertips to talk about if the conversation lags. If you ask a question or raise a subject and he doesn't respond, just let it go. Remember, he's probably just as uncomfortable about dating as you are.

Women have a certain amount of control when dating. They usually have a choice as to where to meet. Some people prefer the intimacy of a good restaurant, one with a nice ambiance. Lunch or dinner is the obvious choice. Others prefer a double date so that the burden of conversation is not entirely on them alone. Before accepting the date, they might want to think about where they'd be most comfortable meeting. Some people prefer the unusual, like a trip to the zoo; others a museum, especially if they like art. One reluctant lady accepted a date with a man because he suggested going horseback riding, and she happened to love horses.

It gives me a feeling of satisfaction when I get two people together, and I always hope something will go further. But sometimes the date doesn't work out. If the man doesn't call back, the woman may call me and ask why. This requires tact, not truth . . . I'll give you an example: a well-educated lady asked me to introduce her to a man I knew. I did. After he went out with her he called me, angry because I had fixed him up "with an irritating, intellectual snob". A few weeks later, she asked me if I knew why he had not called her again. I told her that he felt she was too intelligent for him and he did not like intelligent women.

Not everyone wants to remarry. A widower in my apartment building approached me and, after hemming and hawing for a while, mentioned that he was ready for marriage and was wondering if I knew someone who would fit his specifications. He wanted someone with a good character, charm, personality, a sense of humor, someone who liked animals, long walks, music, and books, someone generous but not a spendthrift.

It just so happened I knew someone who fitted this description perfectly. As soon as he left, I ran to the phone and told her about this "ideal catch: good looking, good character, financially well-to-do, pleasant personality, nice conversationalist." When I finished she said, "Thanks, but no thanks. At this stage in my life I am comfortable with myself. I have good friends and children I love. I don't want to cater to anyone else's whims. I don't want to spend time being nice to somebody else's children and grandchildren. And I don't want to end up being a caretaker. Thank you for thinking of me, but try someone else."

I respected her decision. She knew what she wanted and what she did not want. So many of the single women I meet don't know what they want or what they need, and they wind up with the wrong person just to escape loneliness.

It's easier to meet people if you live in a large apartment building. You meet them at the mailbox, in the lobby, and if you know somebody in the building, they can introduce you to others. If someone is going to the parking lot at the same time you are, you can greet him or her with a smile and "Good morning."

I love people, and I love life. Life is a gift and I treasure every minute of it. I always tell my husband, "We are so blessed. The day is beautiful. We live in a beautiful apartment, and we can do what we want to do. We're blessed." As my mother used to say, "Life is God's gift and if you're not aware of it, shame on you!" She taught me values. She taught me to look at a person's background and home environment because that influences the way people act and approach life. For her, the most important word was character.

My mother was a highly educated woman who spoke seven languages. She taught me that sometimes a husband needs a good word. So every now and then. I use this little phrase from a comic strip that my husband likes, "You're a good man, Charlie Brown." He smiles and answers, "I try, I try."

I have learned something that I did not know when I was younger, and it can be summed up in two words: anticipate and attitude. Anticipate is the word that helped me most in life. Whenever I have to make a decision, I anticipate the consequences, and this helped me avoid a lot of problems.

My second favorite word is attitude. If your attitude is positive, it will help create a positive result. If your attitude is negative, the probability is a negative result. This has been my experience.

I don't really have any fantasies. But when I was a little girl, I used to imagine myself dressed in a long flowing white gown, a beautiful fluffy pink boa, and a sparkling diamond tiara. I held a wand in my hand and every time I waved it my mother had to give me whatever I wanted. That was a nice fantasy.

I think epitaphs should be very simple because the only people for whom an epitaph would have any meaning would be your own family, and they already know you for who you are. I would have a very simple one, like "A devoted mother, a devoted friend, and loving." I would like to be remembered as a giving person. If I were to meet God, I would like Him to say that He respects what I have done in life, which was to raise three very nice children.

This interview reminded me of the days long ago when I used to love "matching up" people. It stopped abruptly when one of the couples I introduced married and then had a very destructive relationship. After that I promised myself I would never, ever matchmake again. Now I'm re-thinking this. There are so many lonely people out there, and every once in a while I see people who I think would be right for each other. I may try again, but this time I will make sure I know more about a person's character and background.

YOUR THOUGHTS:

_____

_____

_____

_____

_____

_____

MARY, THE SHAMPOO LADY

I've been going to the same beauty salon for years where the same shampoo lady usually washes my hair. Mary was one of the invisible people in my life, someone I say hello to, perhaps exchange a few pleasant words with, then go on to something else. One day I really looked at her and saw what was always there, contentment and a sense of calmness. I wondered what Mary was like as a person . . . This is what I learned:

Now that I am older, I am more experienced in life spiritually and emotionally. When I was younger I learned to take life as it comes. Certain things in life are beyond control. I learned to pray more.

I'm not afraid of getting older. Life brings changes every day. With age comes wisdom and knowledge. I thank God for living to this age. I am able to spend a lot of time with my grandchildren. They bring me a lot of happiness and love, and I am more relaxed around them.

Money is very important and nice at any age, young or old. When I look back at my life, though, my health and strength and happiness are more important than money. Money can't buy health and happiness. I haven't found them in any store yet. I look, but don't find them. My mother used to say that manners will take you where money won't. But I realized when I got to the train, that I had manners but no money. I still needed money to board the train.

The best advice I remember getting was from my mother. She told me when I was very young, "Respect others the same way you want to be respected."

I am most proud of being blessed by God, the accomplishments of my daughters, and my granddaughter who is graduating from college. I enjoy spending time with my family and grandchildren. I don't travel too far, because I don't want to fly.

I also enjoy going to church, having dinner and shopping with friends. We go out to dinner so that we can sit and talk. When they start taking our plates away, we know it's time to leave.

I'm glad I took the time to get to know Mary so that she's no longer one of the invisible people in my life. I wonder if there are other people who I would like to get to know on a different level. I have to think about it.

YOUR THOUGHTS:

LITA, THE POLITICIAN

What makes someone want to be a politician? What is the driving force? And how does a wife and mother succeed in politics? How does she integrate so many different aspects into one life? I asked Lita, a popular commissioner in my district and state legislator. This is what she told me about her life and achievements:

My mother was one of eight children, but I am an only child. An unmarried aunt and bachelor uncle lived with us for a while when I was a child. My uncle and my mother had the greatest influence on me. Billy Banks was my uncle's name. He founded two radio stations and a television station. He hired both the first African-American and the first woman on radio in America. My uncle taught me fairness, the importance of community service, and non-bigotry.

My mother was just an extraordinary woman. She was probably one of the first "liberated" women—the only one of six sisters not only to finish high school but also to earn both a Bachelor's degree and a Masters in education. One of her sayings was, "Women are people, too, and I'm a 'people' so I can do anything that a man can do except dig ditches." She taught me the necessity and the mandate to give back because we were given the gift of good brains and comfortable circumstances. My mother instilled in me a love for Judaism and for people. From her, I learned that the glass is half full, not half empty.

Now she has a forty-year-old mind trapped in a 100-year-old body. She still tries to hold on to her independence. She taught me to have independence, the necessity to accomplish, to be somebody, and to serve—and that is who I am.

If I had to describe myself, I would say I'm 'a bull in a china shop' and what you see is what you get. I think my tinted red hair fits my personality. I'm outspoken and very impatient about injustice. I don't let injustice ride. My son once told me, "You can't cure the world." And my response was, "But I'm sure going to try."

My uncle was a founder of the Republican Party in Pennsylvania in 1918, and my father was probably the only Jew who never voted for Roosevelt. He had four chances but never did—so genetically, I am a Republican. We talked a lot about politics at home, and when I was in the sixth grade, I headed the Eisenhower campaign in my school. That is how I got started and became active in Republican Party affairs. In college I was the Pennsylvania vice president of the Young Republicans.

I became active in the county and held party offices. In 1973, when I was appointed to the township planning commission, I became the first woman ever appointed to any commission in Lower Merion. I served for twelve years, ran for commissioner, and served for eight years. Then I ran for the State House and served ten years. I was fortunate to have a mentor, a Federal judge who was a woman.

I am most proud of improving the quality of life of my constituents. That includes so many of my bills that became law and my individual service and caring for people. It is mind boggling to me that I have touched and sometimes helped thousands of people, not only by providing them with the basic necessities of life, like food and heat, but also with life saving measures. Three examples come to mind:

The most glaring example started with a phone call from a woman who said, "You are my last call. I'm going to kill myself." I immediately assigned the three people in my office to call every local, county, and state service organization, and the police, of course, before I quickly drove to her house. When I arrived, the police were already there. She had a gun and was ready to kill herself.

We had just passed welfare reform, which I am proud to state, I had voted against. It required people on welfare to work twenty hours a week if they wanted to continue receiving welfare. This suicidal woman could not do that. She had custody of her dead sister's teenage children and was going to college full-time to better herself so that she could get off welfare. She therefore couldn't work the required twenty hours a week. She was also suffering from schizophrenia, but was taking her medication.

I was able to get a special dispensation from the twenty-hour work mandate and got her all kinds of social service help. Over the years, I've kept in touch with her. Sometimes I sent her flowers. At other times, I would just go and join her for a cup of coffee. She is now thriving, and I am very proud of that.

The second example was a frantic call from the mother of a teenage girl who had run away and was trapped in a drug house. The mother begged me to get her child out of there. I went with the police and rescued the daughter, and I got help for the whole family. This girl and her family are now on the right track.

The third example began when two men came into my office and told me about a homeless neighbor who was very ill and living in his car. He claimed to be a veteran but had no papers or proof of military service. He badly needed medical help. It took two weeks, but we were finally able to get the proof needed, and we got him into a veteran's hospital. He died shortly afterwards, but at least he was in a facility where he received good treatment and did not have to die alone in his car.

These cases just go on and on, and they satisfy me because they make me feel that I am fulfilling my mission in life. These experiences also taught me that my father was wrong. He was a mathematical genius who grew up very poor. As the saying goes, he "pulled himself up by his own boot straps." That is kind of a Republican philosophy—that individuals can help themselves. But my experience in politics taught me empathy, patience, and the mandate that I can never stop giving and helping—and, of course, that many people cannot help themselves and need the government to help them.

My husband is beyond supportive and my children are, too. I think that I succeeded as a parent. The proof is that my son is a lawyer who gave up megabucks at a Wall Street law firm to become a Federal public defender. My daughter is a vice-president of a major credit card company and a community activist.

I tell people, women in particular; that my husband taught me "Never take yourself too seriously" and "It takes fewer muscles to smile then to frown." I think that a positive attitude can cure nearly every ill and conquer almost anything.

Other than losing twenty pounds and being thin, my fantasies have changed during the years. My early fantasy was that I would like to be the wife of a senator; then I realized I would rather be a senator. Now I'm just content to have been what I was and to be what I am now. I do a lot of things to enjoy life. I love getting up in the morning. I hate exercising, but I do it an hour every day. I love being with people, learning, reading, playing the piano, ice-skating, needlepoint, and laughing. I love to laugh. And of course I love being with my grandchildren.

I look forward to good health, long life, watching my grandchildren grow up, and hopefully making the world a better place where people can live well without war and in a healthy, environmentally safe society.

In difficult times, my anger takes over. I really am a very angry person in my determination to correct evil and wrong. Religion plays an enormous role in my life, and I became more aware of this in my ten years in the legislature. I was the only Jew in the majority caucus, and I learned that my way of thinking and approach to issues was based upon my Judaism and was very often different from the Christian world. And my sense of right and wrong is really dictated by Judaism's standards.

I would like my epitaph to read: "She wanted it all." I would like to be remembered as being gorgeous and brilliant—and that I always gave my best. I would like to say to God, "Send me back. There is more to do."

The word "politician" often has a negative connotation. Listening to Lita, I was reminded that there are sincere and caring people in politics who really want to make a difference and often do so. It's good to be reminded . . .

YOUR THOUGHTS:

_____

_____

_____

_____

_____

_____

LAURIE, THE THEATRE PRODUCER

Everyone is born with gifts. Some people develop their gifts; others waste them. Blessed with talent, creativity, and an entrepreneurial spirit, Laurie has used her gifts to make a major impact in the world of musical theatre in the United States. She is a producer, an entrepreneur, and an educator. Her story . . . .

I founded my company thirty-five years ago. It's the nation's leading producer of musical theater for families and children and presents award-winning musicals in over 400 cities throughout the United States. We have twenty-four tours each year in America and Canada and even overseas if requested. We perform anywhere from large theaters to school auditoriums. Our annual attendance is 1.4 million people.

I am very proud of what we have accomplished. Yet it seems so far away from thirty or forty years ago. At that time, had you asked me to tell you what I did, I would have said, "I'm a mother and a teacher." Making brownies with my young daughters on cold winter afternoons so many years ago were among the happiest days of my life.

One of the things that has helped me succeed is the ability to focus, to be in the present moment. When I'm with my grandchildren, I'm Gram. When I am with my husband, I am his wife, friend, and lover. When I'm here in my office, I'm a producer. I have written eight original musicals and have commissioned and produced forty-six musicals. That is what I have been doing the last thirty-five years.

I am the product of input from so many people. I have digested some of the input. Other input I have either been unable or unwilling to accept. When I started my production company, someone said, "How foolish! What a waste of time." The fact is that my impact on the arts and education in America has been profound.

I don't think of myself as a creative entity. I just put one foot in front of another. My mother used to say, "Beauty is as beauty does." I expand that to say, "Talent is as talent does and creativity is as creativity does." You may have all this in you, but if you don't put it to work, it's meaningless. How it plays out—that is what it's about.

I enjoy life. I walk, I travel. I love opera and film. I love being with my husband, my kids, and my grandchildren. And here's the newest—I started to knit. When my daughter heard that she said, "You're kidding!" Anything I do better gives me joy.

I'm grateful to be vertical. I'm grateful that those I love are physically well. I look forward to . . . more. Life contains many sweet moments. Some of these sweet moments are simple; some are convoluted. I appreciate them all—that is why I want more.

I used to have a ballet fantasy, and every time I go to the ballet I still turn green with envy at the beauty and skill of the ballerinas. If I were to have a fantasy now, I'd get on with it—not wait.

What I've learned now that I am older is that life is not a straight line. It has its ups and downs. I know that when you are down physically, financially, or emotionally, if you have the energy and the courage to stay alive, you will see another sunny day.

What advice do I have for others? If I would dare give advice, I would say: Set your priorities, but allow them to change periodically. Also, exercise; eat correctly; and practice moderation—if you can. Participate in the arts and in the gardens of your life, too.

I love the old tunes that we sing during the holidays, and I enjoy the traditions, but religion does not play a major role in my life. I believe that God and nature are one. I am touched by children. I think children are a life force. It is their very neediness that keeps us alive. Their vulnerability is a responsibility, and we need responsibility in order to grow.

In difficult times, my husband's savvy optimism and generosity of spirit sustain me. And I have learned from my sister, who is a cornerstone of my life, that if I can get through a difficult period, a bright day will be waiting ahead.

At my funeral, I do not want speeches, only music by Vivaldi, Lully, and Kreisler. On my epitaph I would like only to have my name and dates of my birth and death. The dates say it all. No one will remember me the same way. Everyone I come in contact with has a different take and different perspective on who I am. Therefore, let them each remember me as they will.

Recently a high school friend of my daughter from many years ago stopped me on the street, identified herself, and said, "I remember coming to your home forty years ago, and you served a crown roast. It was the most wonderful thing I had ever seen. I will never forget it and will never forget you for serving so beautifully." That is how this woman remembers me, and that is just fine with me.

I feel that life is a series of vignettes. When you put them all together, you have a tale. When the time comes, I would like God to say, "Welcome. Come inside. We have some great adventures up ahead." Regretfully, even tragically, I do not believe in any form of continuity after death. I desperately wish I did.

In each chapter of Laurie's life, she is able to live in the moment, to be fully present and focused. It is a trait that many of us need to learn. I admire her love of life and sense of play that is contagious. She is not only an innovator and leader of musical theatre, but also a person you can imagine running in the park, flying a kite, followed by little children, laughing—and I would love to be part of that scene, flying a great big red balloon. I came away from this conversation with Laurie realizing that I love being with creative people, and I need to spend more time with friends who are fun.

YOUR THOUGHTS:

_____

_____

_____

_____

_____

_____

AGNES, THE UNFULFILLED WOMAN

For me, the saddest two words in the English language are "if only." When we think of the past, it is often hard to let go. It's only human to think, "If only I had . . . " or "If only something else had happened . . . " Sadly, the "if onlys" can color the present and our hopes for the future. I was reminded of this when I struck up a conversation with the receptionist while waiting to see my dentist. I asked Agnes how she became a dental receptionist and this is her story:

I'm not what I could have been. My mother died when I was seven, and I did not want to go to school. I just couldn't get my mind to focus on schoolwork. My father married again, and my stepmother was mean to me.

I should have furthered my education. I could have gone to school and made something of myself. I always wanted to own a little boutique. I have good taste and know I could have been successful at it. But everyone told me it was the wrong time to go into business, and I listened to them. Whenever I brought it up again, it was never the right time.

I lived with my sister and brother-in-law although I wanted to be on my own. But everyone said, "You can't be on your own," so I got married. That was the biggest mistake of my life. I had a bad marriage. I did not know enough about him. There were so many secrets that I did not know. When we came home from our honeymoon, he sat me down in the kitchen and told me things that so disgusted me that I left him.

I became a dental receptionist because I didn't want to go to college, and that was the first job I got. Somehow the years flew by, and I am still a dental receptionist, but it was never what I wanted to be. I had so much talent. I knit beautifully and make one-of-a-kind sweaters. I crochet baby clothes that are nicer than anything you can buy in a store, and people usually tell me that my cakes and cookies are the best they ever tasted. I made a cornucopia last week out of breadsticks that was the hit of a party. Everyone *raved* about it. So what! It doesn't put money in the bank. I tried to sell my cakes to stores, but I use the best ingredients and can't produce quantity in my small kitchen, so it would not have been a paying proposition.

People always compliment me on my excellent taste in clothes. I don't pay much for them, but I have a good eye for detail and can always spot a bargain. I wanted to work as a buyer of women's clothing in a department store, but whenever I applied for an interview in a department store, they wouldn't see me because I didn't have credentials or experience.

An accountant once gave me some good advice: "Put all your savings in stocks." I did, and I made some really good money, enough for a down payment on a condominium. When I told the accountant what I planned to do, he advised me against it. I listened to him. The stocks went down. I lost 40 percent of my savings and could no longer afford the down payment.

Someone sent me a New Year's card on which was written, "It's never too late to be what you might have been. (George Elliot). Is it possible for you to achieve that illusive goal?" It sounds good, but I don't believe it's true for me.

On the other hand, I feel very lucky because I have a wonderful sister and two supportive brothers. I adore my nephews and nieces and can't do enough for them. When times are difficult, I know I can depend on my family.

My church used to be a great comfort to me. My father was a staunch Catholic, and my happiest memories were his holding my hand and going with him to church. I miss it. But when my brother was getting remarried and I was invited to be the Matron of Honor, my priest told me I could not attend because my brother was divorced. I went to the wedding anyway but stopped going to church. I still feel I'm a Catholic, and I pray at home, but it's not the same.

The best advice I could give others is to tell them that, if they have a dream, they should work for it. So many things are not what they should be. I shouldn't have listened to people. I should have followed my dream and opened a boutique. I could have sold my handmade things there, even had a little counter for cookies and cakes. I would have loved it. I would have thrived. It hurts whenever I think of it. I'm sorry. I just can't talk about it any more. It's too painful.

Then she got up and walked away. It is painful when dreams are squashed. I know! Years ago my best friend's son told me he planned to take the money his parents had saved for his education and open a restaurant. My reaction was, "WHAT? You are going to take your parents' hard-earned money and lose it in the restaurant business? Most new restaurants go bankrupt within the first year. You know nothing about the business . . . ."

Had I to do it now, my approach would be different: "You sound excited, tell me about it." Then I would ask him to tell me his concerns. I would have added mine, and together we might have come to a positive conclusion . . . perhaps he could apply to a restaurant school . . . or speak first with people who had opened up successful restaurants . . . Whatever the result, at least he would have explored his dream and made his own decision. He is now a business administrator, hates his job, and every once in a while he tells me, "If only I hadn't listened to you, I . . . . " It does hurt!

YOUR THOUGHTS:

_____

_____

_____

_____

_____

_____

PETUNIA, THE PROBLEM SOLVER

I admire people who get a lot done yet seem to have enough time for everything—someone like my friend Petunia. I admire her tremendously. She's the perfect friend in need. Whenever you need her, she's there for you. Need a plumber? Can't find a handyman? Need a listening ear? Call Petunia. She inspires confidence, admiration, and trust, while keeping relationships in a healthy balance. How does she do it?

I'm called Awesome Petunia because I tend to use the word "awesome" a lot. I would describe myself as full of energy, with a passion for fun. I have a wonderful family, a job that I love, and a husband who appreciates me.

I am known to be task-oriented. I know what needs to be done and thrive on the challenge of completing tasks within a designated timeframe. Without a doubt, mornings are my best time. I strongly believe in finding the easiest, least time consuming way to accomplish tasks. I live by multitasking. I am always doing two or more things at the same time. This is more out of necessity and survival, but it can have pros and cons. I love to entertain and find it rather easy to pull meals together quickly. I think people just want to get together and are not really interested in the hostess killing herself and being exhausted by the time they arrive.

I plan ahead of time and make a list of the foods I plan to serve. I then make a food shopping list insuring that I have all the ingredients necessary. You would be surprised how using some foods that are already prepared and adding your own little touch makes things so much easier. If it is important to use the good china, I put it in the dishwasher. Silver survives the dishwasher as long as it is separated from stainless. I clean the pots as we go along and prepare as much of the meal as I can beforehand.

As I reflect back on family holidays, I laugh out loud at some of the unusual things that occurred. One year, my uncle demonstrated karate on a watermelon. We all were covered with seeds, including the ceiling. Then there was the Thanksgiving when my daughter removed her grandmother's dessert plate from the table and later realized she had also taken her false teeth. Her grandmother hadn't noticed that they had fallen out. No one laughed harder than Granny when she found out.

Another year, when the turkey was taken out of the oven, we discovered that the oven had never been turned on. If you take the time to look back, you will be amazed at what really matters. Try to remember that and spend your time accordingly.

When I was younger and even more energetic, I assumed that everyone had the same quickness and energy that I had. It effected my communication and relationships. I used to worry about everything being perfect. When I had two little children and was working full-time, my house was perfect. When I had my third child, I realized how silly it was to spend all that energy and time on housework. You can really intimidate your friends when everything has to be just so. I still want things to look nice, but it isn't unusual for things to be "untidy." When you visit someone, who really does a "white glove" test?

My friends will often tell you how interesting my life is. Every week I can entertain friends with the bizarre events that happened to me. I can honestly say, looking back, I really have "bad luck." We have had floods in the kitchen that have spilled into the basement, broken bones at the worst times, floods in the basement the day of a christening, accidents involving both of our cars at the same time—just to name a few. From these experiences, we have learned to laugh a lot (and cry, too). We have also learned to put things in perspective. If it can be fixed, we are lucky!

I am not a visionary person. I would say "realistic" would be more appropriate. My credo is "Never take more than you give." By this I mean that in all aspects of your life, make sure you are giving more of yourself or giving back more to your environment than you take from it. You need to give more to your relationships than you take. If you live by this rule, you will never leave things out of balance.

I have an awesome group of friends who are always there for each other. I am very proud of this and grateful that I can be of help to them. Friends come to me all the time and tell me their problems. They know I would never repeat their troubles and feel confident that together we can find a practical solution. I think that the best thing I can do for friends is to listen. People don't want you to solve their problems. They need to arrive at their own answers, but I can help my friends by doing research for them. Resources can be tapped to assist the situation. For example, I have a dear friend who was having a problem with both depression and guilt after her husband died. She was also concerned about all the medicines she was taking. I went online and got detailed information about the medications and their possible side effects. This empowered her to go back to her doctor and discuss her concerns. Maybe that is it—we need to feel empowered to take control of the situation. Wow! I like that.

Another friend stays in an abusive relationship. We can listen to her and try to give some suggestions, but ultimately it is her choice to stay or leave. If leaving is not her option, then friends need to make sure she has the necessary resources available to handle an emergency situation. She needs to know where to go and how to get there fast. If she decides to leave and needs to explore how she can best do it, I strongly urge her to be very cautious. If her husband finds out that she plans to leave him, it could have dangerous consequences.

Sometimes a friend begins to take advantage of friends, or it just becomes too much. It is easier said than done, but the best advice is to nip it in the bud. Unfortunately, often you don't realize that you are digging yourself in too deep until you are six feet under. Then what? Well, I have found from experience that honesty is the best policy. You need to let friends know that, though you are there for them, they may need additional help that you cannot offer.

You have the choice to be miserable and stay in this relationship or be upfront and let them know that you have no more to offer. You need to go back to my credo—"Never take more than you give." If you feel that your friend is taking more than she is giving, it is time to reevaluate the friendship and reevaluate what each is contributing. It may seem harsh, but if it's a true friendship, both sides will benefit from an upfront, honest conversation in the long run.

People often ask me what I do for myself. Two things: I always work out and I always try to get my sleep. I truly believe that I need to get eight hours sleep a night. If I don't, I let things bother me that normally I could rationalize and put in perspective. I exercise and love to workout every day!! Running is one of my favorite coping devices. When I feel down or tired, I go running and then feel reenergized and ready to face anything.

I have my challenges. I'm a high-energy person, but some other people in my life are not. They like moving at a slow pace and enjoy relaxing in front of a TV. That used to drive me crazy. I'm now much better at understanding various energy levels and individual styles. My husband and I are very different. He's very laid back. He tends to be a visionary and thinks things through. (I consider this over-analyzing.) I often jump into things quickly just to get them done.

Together we are perfect, but that doesn't mean we don't have our issues during the process. Trust me, there have been times when I have said "Hello, where are you? You are not following me." I might push him more than he would like, but he also makes me think things through more than I would on my own. When we were first married, I became a bit frustrated with my husband and used to head-on in for a fight. Now I am more understanding. I need to remember to take a deep breath and listen to what he has to say—again, easier said than done; but it does prevent some wicked battles.

Family is one of my cherished blessings. I was raised by two of the most AWESOME parents in the world. I have a wonderful sister and two great brothers. My sister is my closest friend and confidant. She knows all my deep, dark secrets. She is the first one I call when I have a problem. We are very lucky to have each other. I know she will always be there for me and vice versus. I have three beautiful children. Each gives my life such meaning. I am forever growing as I see things through their eyes during different stages of their lives. They are also a great resource of information. They have great insight and keep things in perspective for me.

Religion is very important to me. I have a very strong faith. My husband is Catholic, and I am Methodist. This has led to some challenging moments in our relationship. I truly believe in a loving, caring God. I can only imagine what He is thinking as he looks down at his children when we debate issues that really are not important in the larger scheme of things. My family and my religion sustain me during difficult times. I have a wonderful support system through my church and my family. No matter what I need to face, I know there is someone waiting to help me through it. I believe in the power of prayer and truly believe that "God only gives us what we can handle." But as the saying goes, "I just wish he didn't trust me so much."

On my epitaph I would like written: "True Friend, Loving Mother and Caring Wife." I would like to be remembered as someone who loved unconditionally and could always be counted on. And when the time comes, I would like God to say, "I am proud of what you have accomplished with the talents I have given you."

There is a lesson here that I needed to learn: how to deal with people who take advantage of me, people who want more then I am willing to give. I tend to avoid confrontation and let the relationship get to the point where it's destructive. I prefer Petunia's solution—it allows for the possibility of keeping the relationship and not feel "used." And of course, the obvious lesson here is—find yourself a friend like Petunia.

YOUR THOUGHTS:

_____

_____

_____

_____

_____

_____

JENNY, THE ADVENTUROUS WOMAN

You can know a person for years but never really see her as she sees herself. I've known Jenny for many years and always thought of her as a pleasant, quiet, unassuming woman. In no way would I have described her as "an adventurer"—but that's the way she described herself. Here's why:

I think of myself as a very private person. I'm a grey-haired woman who gets around some, but not too much, and who doesn't spend much time on her appearance. I'm interested in people, but I have trouble making the first approach. I feel perhaps I should be more outgoing toward others.

When I contrast my past with my present life, I see how I have become more of an adventurer. After I graduated from college, I entered hospital training for a specific laboratory and was married—all within three months. I entered the laboratory field before it was fully recognized. Perhaps that was the first hint of an adventurous spirit within me.

In my professional life, I worked in a specialized lab, which meant working within a very narrow range and leading a rather restricted life. I became a supervisor, but the hospital did not allow more than two weeks vacation at one time. We spent this time visiting family and never truly explored our own country.

My husband was in industry before he began teaching at a university. He teaches computer sciences. Now we live by the academic calendar and are free all summer and one month in winter. My husband and I made a decision that we can live where we are on our basic income even though we have been gradually spending down our savings by traveling. Our children approve of our spending their inheritance. I started looking at places to visit. For some reason, Costa Rica caught my fancy first. I don't know why. It had something to do with the way the vegetation and the countryside were described. That was our first trip.

When I retired, another couple asked us to join them on a four-week celebration trip exploring Alaska. We extended the trip by visiting family in Oregon and California. We had never been away for an extended period of time. It was probably the beginning of the "adventurous lady."

Alaska was such an incredible experience that we just wanted to keep on traveling. The following summer, my husband became very ill and we were not able to travel. When he recovered, we immediately started planning the next trip. Going somewhere for five weeks really freed us up. Simply the thought that we did not have to be around the house, that we could go places, was freeing. Once we got the taste of the freedom of travel, we wanted to continue.

Our next trip was to China, but it ended abruptly when I fell the first day. I tried to continue the trip by denying any serious injury, but two days after the fall, I realized my arm should be x-rayed. It was broken and I had to go home very quickly. The next year we went back to China and got through the entire three weeks. It was a fascinating experience to see a new culture and a country that was booming and changing.

Another year we decided to see more of our own country. We followed the route of Lewis and Clark on a special bus trip—the initial run by Elder Hostel exploring that route. We had the advantage of being accompanied by the person who conceived the idea of following Lewis and Clark. Minor disadvantages included picnic stops that had closed for repairs. But a cemetery provided an alternate eating area, and Wal-Mart provided an alternate rest stop. We saw the countryside from the bus and appreciated it so much more than when we flew over it.

The following year we visited Israel and Italy, and this past year we went to Africa. Our next trip to will be to India because my husband has had a lot of students from India.

An odd way to measure the way I've changed as a traveler is my approach to restrooms. When I went to China, I was always looking for Western style restrooms. On last year's trip to Africa, when there was a lineup at the Western style restroom, I just used the more primitive hole in the restroom floor. That was when I realized that my traveling views had changed. My son has been in Uzbekistan on a business trip, and one of the pictures he sent by e-mail was a similar kind of facility that he kept coming across during his trip.

Life has taught me that I might as well try new things. Simply waiting at home isn't any safer or better than what's out there in the rest of the world. People sometimes ask us," Why are you flying to such far out, dangerous places?" I replied by quoting statistics about more people being killed in automobiles than on planes or trips abroad. The Israelis have the same approach. When my husband and I visited Israel, we asked about terrorists. The Israelis responded by asking us, "How many people are killed by violence in your cities?" That approach has been imbedded in me since then.

If I had to give one bit of advice, I would say, "Try new things." Like playing the piano. About fifteen years ago, someone I worked with was selling an old piano. I paid more for moving it and tuning it than I paid for the piano itself. I started piano lessons because I had always felt that there was something missing in my life—the ability to make music. l have discovered I have very little talent, but I have improved and keep playing.

When I'm home I like reading *The New York Times*. We have subscriptions to the Metropolitan Opera in New York and the Philadelphia Ballet. We go to Washington for the Shakespeare Theater. We wander through museums— especially the art museums. It makes up for all the years when we only went to science, space and natural history museums with our children.

I have been grounded in the sciences too long to indulge in fantasies, so I have none to share. I do hope and look forward to continued good health so I can continue doing what I have been doing.

A basic faith and a community of friends sustain me during difficult times. Religion plays a role in my life as a sort of underlying piece. Its underneath—it comes up when there is a need; when I need some way to keep going. I never think about things like epitaphs or how I would like to be remembered, and certainly not what God would say to me. But if pressed, I would probably like something nice on my epitaph, along the lines of "She helped others and enjoyed her life." How I would like to be remembered? I can't think of anything except clichés. And if God were to speak with me, I would like Him to say something like, "You did a lot with your life and helped others along the way."

Although most of her early life was quietly traditional, Jenny became more adventurous over the years and mastered the art of living well—pursuing her passion for travel and making time for her interests. I wonder if it started when Jenny asked herself what was missing in her life and began filling the gap with piano lessons, which became the first of other new interests?

YOUR THOUGHTS:

_____

_____

_____

_____

_____

_____

ROMANA, THE SURVIVOR

Despite one calamity after another throughout her life, Romana not only survives but manages to retain a "joie de vivre." She enjoys fine food, opera, travel, and entertaining loved ones and friends. I wanted to know more about her life and how she has achieved serenity and harmony.

I was born on the Italian-Istrian peninsula in 1943, just as the Axis powers began their slide to defeat. This area and most cities on the Ilyrian coast have always been buffeted by war and political changes. My parents were born there before World War I. We left with an estimated 250,000 other immigrants when the area was ceded to Yugoslavia in 1946, but we chose to retain our Italian identity. My family resettled north of Milan where my father had a desk job in the post office.

Post war life was difficult, and we were not economically comfortable. At the urging of one of my father's sisters, who had immigrated to the United States in 1912, my parents decided to take advantage of the United States Displaced Persons Act. We arrived in New York in 1951 after a wintry weeklong crossing aboard a troop transfer ship. We rode a train to East Chicago, Indiana, a harbor section close to the steel mills that attracted untold numbers of others in similar circumstances.

The next ten years proved very difficult for my parents as they struggled in their new surroundings. They eventually achieved a comfortable lower-middle-class life but lacked the support and camaraderie of their families and the comfort of their own culture. Both worked full time—my father at Inland Steel and my mother in a men's clothing factory. As they adapted to American life, I remember many emotions of frustration, sadness, and loneliness, but also humor, hope, happiness, and satisfaction.

After the initial bewilderment of the drastic changes in lifestyle and culture, my brother and I quickly adapted and became all-American teenagers—with the added distinction that we drank wine with our meals! Thanks to good genes and parental urging, we completed university studies. Despite the hardships of my early years, I remember the warmth and love I received from my parents. Even as I went through my teen years and began to see the human, sometimes flawed aspects of their personalities, I was aware of the enormity of their struggles.

The ultimate irony, however, was that first my mother and later my father succumbed to Alzheimer's disease at relatively young ages. Both lived many years in the twilight of dementia where they could not appreciate and enjoy what they, their children, and grandchildren had achieved as a result of their life's difficult journey.

Two events of my adult life have been the most painful. One was the death of my first-born child who was born with a faulty heart. After much hope and prayers, he died when he was two-years-old. At the beginning of his medical journey, I cried a lot, of course. But I noticed that when I cried, I became quite unwell with headaches and thus less capable of taking care of him. I realized that my crying was really self-indulgent and selfish because he was the one who was ill and needed my strength.

At his death there was so much to do. Both sets of grandparents needed comforting, my friends were devastated, and I had had another child, eight-month-old Nicole, who needed my care, which was a comfort to me. So I went on automatic pilot when people were around. I did cry privately with my husband. We talked through our pain and accepted the reality that having had our little boy for the short time we did was a gift.

The second event was making the decision to admit my mother to a nursing home. In her dementia, she was overcome by sudden rages towards my father and me. She swung at us in anger at unpredictable moments. One day she forgot who her seven-year-old grandson was. I came upon her threatening to hit him because she felt he was mocking her by not speaking to her in Italian. This was the deciding incident. I could not chance that any more of her outbursts might harm my child. I realized that she needed constant supervision, and I could no longer be responsible for her care in my own home. My mother, who had been such a beautiful, bright, kind woman, had undergone such sad changes. In essence, she had shed the qualities that shaped her personality.

Of the many events that shaped my life, those two events were the low points and pivotal to me, but I believe they actually gave me strength. They were equally painful, yet I viewed them slightly differently. I saw my son's death as an act of God, but moving my mother out of my home was my choice. The night before I took her to the nursing home was almost worse than my child's death because I was choosing to no longer care for the woman who had given me birth and had so lovingly cared for me. I felt that was abdicating my duty as a daughter. I did not sleep that night.

I've survived other sorrows, some of which have turned out well. My young husband was an alcoholic, but he learned to cope and achieve sobriety. Jack has remained sober for twenty-six years.

My lovely eleven-year-old daughter Nicole was diagnosed with *dermatomyositis*, a disease related to lupus. For four years, she was so weakened that she had to use a wheelchair and be home-schooled intermittently. The disease caused a chain of other problems, including a deep depression that undermined her progress in high school. She eventually overcame her illnesses, finished college and law school, married, and is settled in her life.

About ten years ago, my teenage son rebelled at the upper-middle-class normality of our family and, in essence, rejected me and the family life I worked so hard to achieve. I continuously had the feeling that he did not receive enough of my love and attention when he was younger because of all these other circumstances in our lives. This breach has thankfully been worked out now that he's older.

Our family living arrangement was rather complex when I engineered what, I thought, was a great solution for everyone. We bought a spacious older home and combined multi-generational households to achieve a situation that I believed would benefit everyone. My parents joined us, and my husband soon had to deal with in-laws in his home. Later his mother moved in with us. It was my choice, but she eventually went to a nursing home when she broke her hip in a fall.

I had initiated this multi-generational, bi-lingual family arrangement because I thought it would be a logical solution for us all. Everyone else, of course, pulled at the restraints of such an arrangement, and I grew continually frustrated that they did not see it as I had envisioned.

Jack had a bout with melanoma cancer and currently is fighting leukemia. I sometimes feel we are just waiting for the other shoe to drop. I've had my own problems with atrial fibrillation, for which I've had two electrocardiac conversions that are much less invasive than operations. I find my particular health problem exquisitely ironic—in essence, my heart developed problems from having to cope with so much!

I don't want to emphasize only the difficult times, however. My life is full of wonderful memories, of smiles, love, gatherings, color, music . . . and my love of and ability in clothing design, which was my intended career prior to falling in love with Jack when I was eighteen. I feel confident that, if I had pursued a career in fashion as a young woman, I would have achieved certain success. But I would have become a different woman, somewhat harsher to be able to survive in that world, I think. Instead, I chose to be a somewhat traditional wife and mother, but that early interest has always been subsurface and served me well with my approach to life. I almost explode with energy when these unused talents are allowed to surface. For example, I am now working with the director of an opera company. But I also am aware that they are using me chiefly because I am cheap labor and willing to do it for the love of music and creativity!

Sometimes I have felt that I was "put upon" by fate and needed to rebel a bit for being taken for granted or continuously postponing what I want to do for myself. About ten years ago, I replenished my soul by spending three months in Italy. I had taken a few Italian classes, and a professor suggested that my Italian was good but rusty. All I had to do, he said, was go to Italy for six months or a year and I'd quickly pick up fluency. I decided that I needed to do just that. I went for three months and had a fantastic experience. I compare it to being the guest of honor at an elaborate banquet. I got to know my relatives, made new friends, learned a lot, and happily returned to my family.

When friends call me a "survivor," I think there must be something deep in my background that has contributed to this trait. Like most Italians, my family enjoys bringing together family and friends to dine, picnic, play cards, and most of all sing. When I recall my childhood, the most frequent image that comes to mind is sitting near one of my parents or on their laps, listening to them and their friends as they played cards, bantered, and sang. I heard so many folk songs, even religious ones, and especially opera pieces. My mother directed the chorus parts while she, an accomplished musician and soprano, sang the melody. Despite the many problems that I have dealt with in life, I really think this memory has provided one of solid planks of my personality and my approach to life. Solace can always be found in friendship and music, which to me are intrinsically tied to religion or spirituality.

My happiest moments now are when I prepare a special meal for family or dear friends or when I plan a social event because that means I will be with people I love or whose company I enjoy. I can give them what I do best, preparing a lovely table, good food, etc. I also enjoy books and music and, of course, Italian opera! Not having the talent to make my own music, I very much appreciate others' talents.

When I think about the best advice anyone ever gave me, it seems that no matter what clever way the advice is given, it always comes back to being aware that one does not know all the facts. I think it's important not to judge quickly because each situation is different. Others' views and circumstances may be better or just different than your own. I think it's good advice to try and see a situation through others' perceptions.

I was reminded of this non-judgmental virtue the other day by this "ah life!" moment: We were in Chicago and stopped at a coffee shop. As we went to a table, we passed a man at a table and I noticed that he was reading a copy of *The DaVinci Code*, the new illustrated one that I had seen in bookstores. The man was seated looking away from me. Curious to look at the book, I leaned towards him and in a friendly voice said, "I see that you're reading *The DaVinci Code?*" No answer. I repeated myself. Again, no answer. I stepped back and thought that he was either very deep in thought or just rude. A few minutes later, his woman companion sat down at his table and I realized that they were quietly gesticulating in sign language. I smiled and once again realized that I'd been reminded to be open to other explanations for what I see and perceive.

As for giving advice, I have often told younger women to appreciate the quiet, routine days of their lives because the highs and lows will come. The quiet days prepare you and provide strength to get through the difficult, stressful times and give you energy for the good times. Of course, the stressful times can also be happy—I'm still smiling over the work that was put into my daughter Nicole's wedding. It was one of the happiest times but ridiculously busy and pleasantly stressful.

Now that I am sixty-one, when difficult situations come along, I can relate them to past events and life lessons (such as memories of my parents' immigration experience and the hard times they endured). This reflection helps me face difficulties more easily. I remind myself that for all *my* perceived problems, my parents had a more difficult time. I also reflect on the good things in my life. Since my marriage I have enjoyed financial security, the comfort of a social milieu, and a good husband who is caring and loving, which I now think are the ideal circumstances to deal with life.

When I was younger, I didn't understand that "time heals all wounds." Now I appreciate that time also smoothes the frictions of life and helps us live with—dare I use the word—wisdom. In looking back over the timeline of our lives, I am amazed to see the high and low points and how events and emotions that sparked such strong passions have now quieted down and devolved into unimportant aspects of our past.

As my children are now launched on their life's journey, I look forward hopefully to sharing or teaching others some of what I have learned. I'd like to teach informally . . . evening courses, perhaps. I also hope to do more traveling. I'd like to be remembered as a good person, a daughter, wife, mother, and friend who was enjoyable to be around, who had some talents and did some things that pleased others.

In heaven, I'd hope God would say to me, "I know you have tried and I understand the reason why you occasionally procrastinated." My secret fault (not so secret to my husband) is my tendency to procrastinate. I have several theories about why I tend in this direction. I have discovered that what has to be done eventually gets done, and oftentimes the peripheral work that accompanies various tasks and duties are unnecessary and do not affect the outcome.

Romana's story reminds me of an old Scottish proverb: "I am wounded, but I am not slain. I shall lay me down and bleed a while, then I shall rise and fight again." Her life has certainly been rich with highs and lows, joys and tragedies, but she has survived—thrived, really—because she loves life. I suspect that this love was planted and nurtured very early in her life by warm, loving parents when they lived in sunny Italy—that and the fact that she loves being with people and continued doing what she enjoys: entertaining, listening to music, being involved in cultural and community activities.

YOUR THOUGHTS:

INTERVIEW WITH ME

Anne, A Woman in Process

I hope you have enjoyed meeting the previous twenty-nine women and have gleaned some of their wisdom, wit, courage, stamina, and zest for life. They are uniquely admirable, don't you think? After I interviewed these women and was preparing this book, I thought that readers might also wonder about me—my life and reflections. I hesitated at first, but then I decided it might be fun to interview myself. It could be of interest to you the reader and possibly a learning experience for me. Here's the result:

I see myself as a woman in the process of becoming more and more of whom I want to be. When I was younger, I chose to go to work rather than finishing college, a decision that seemed sensible at a time when things were financially tough. While I don't regret that decision—what's done is done—I used to have an inordinate respect for the opinions of people who had university degrees. Then I went back to school in my mid-forties, got my Bachelor and Master degrees, and realized that a piece of paper did not make people intellectually superior.

When I was a young bride, I was very disorganized and used to envy people who managed to work and get everything done. A few years later I discovered self-help books and learned better organizational skills. I'm still far from perfect, but with my "to-do" list, I manage to get more things done and avoid last minute pressure.

Most of all, I admired those thin, energetic, disciplined people who exercised and resisted tempting desserts. I'm still not thin, but with time I became more and more aware of preventive medicine and the importance of maintenance. So while I don't always want to, I make time for exercise and, given the choice between an apple and apple cake, I often choose the apple and enjoy it.

I used to admire gourmet cooks and never believed I could become one. I was right. At this stage of my life, however, my guests sometimes appreciate low cholesterol meals and in turn I look forward to being invited to dinner by gourmet cooks and enjoying their sumptuous, who-cares-about-calories dinners. One of the nice things about getting older is giving up old aspirations and settling for what is—and enjoying it.

In essence, I think of myself as an easygoing person, someone who loves to laugh and enjoys people but who also has a need to be alone sometimes and reflect. The key word in my life right now is "gratitude." I feel so fortunate to be in good health and that my husband and children are all well. Now that my children are grown, I very much appreciate that I have the freedom to make more choices about living my own life.

I enjoy so many things. Walking, learning, and crossing things off my "to do" list give me pleasure. I love to listen to classical music with my husband. I love communicating with my children and grandchildren. And at this stage in my life, it is so nice to take a morning off occasionally to read, take a walk, or just do nothing without feeling guilty about it.

One of the key experiences in my adult life was going back to school in my mid-forties. This marked the beginning of my quest to explore my own being, as opposed to focusing only on being a good wife, mother, daughter, and friend. I decided to get a degree in counseling because of an incident that troubled me.

A friend was critically ill and I went to visit her in the hospital. When she saw me she cried out, "Anne, I'm dying."

"No, Stella," I responded. "You can't think like that. Your children need you. Your husband needs you."

"My husband will marry again. I lost all my hair. I'm dying."

I tried to persuade her to be more positive, but nothing I said changed her mind or brought her comfort. I left feeling sad and discouraged. I had so wanted to make her feel better. As I lay awake in bed that night, I realized I had not met her need to talk or discuss her fears. I could not handle her pain. A few weeks later, I returned to see her and was told she had died. I could not forgive myself for not "being there" for a friend when she needed me. So when I went back to college, I worked toward a counseling degree so that I would learn how to communicate better and help people.

I learned four things at university: the importance of research; the necessity of doing homework; the fact that some people will see you in a way you don't see yourself; and not to quit when you are discouraged because you may regret it.

These were not happy learning experiences. For me, doing research was intimidating. It took a good year before I felt comfortable in the huge, impersonal university library. And I hated doing homework. My stomach literally ached when I tried to comprehend difficult textbooks. I desperately wanted to do well and get good marks so I would not be ashamed when my husband and children asked to see my grades.

Some teachers, who were younger than I, found an older student intimidating. I first realized this when I asked one professor how to study for an exam. There was so much material and I didn't want to do unnecessary work. He looked at me coldly and said, "Please, Anne, don't try to con me." Evidently I looked like I knew it all.

Another incident occurred when I attended a Group Interaction class. I liked the course and felt comfortable participating. One intellectual-looking young student who had never spoken in class was told by the teacher to participate or she would fail him. To make it even more difficult for him, she asked him to stand, find one person whom he disliked, and tell that to him or her. I looked around to see who that person was and found him pointing at ME!.

"But why?" I asked. "Have I said something to offend you?"

"No."

"Did I say anything in class that bothered you?"

"No."

"Then why do you dislike me?"

"It's the way you're dressed. You always look so perfect. You're just like my Aunt Clara, always perfect, always telling me what to do, never able to take a joke."

"But I only take time to dress well because I need that extra confidence . . ." And I stopped. I realized that no matter what I said, he would still see me as his miserable Aunt Clara.

Being older has its advantages. Had that incident occurred when I was younger, I would have been devastated. The next day, I wore jeans and an old tee shirt to class.

That experience taught me the importance of image and led to my writing a book on projecting the image one wants to convey. It also made me realize that I had to work on not taking it personally when people say hurtful things.

School became easier after I learned the ropes, but three months before getting my degree I decided to quit because I felt I would not be a good counselor. My husband persuaded me to continue until I got my degree. I'm glad I listened to him because, had I quit before getting it, I would have felt like a failure. As part of the counseling experience, I attended seminars and found that I was focusing on humor and the importance of laughter in diffusing anxiety. So I took courses on humor therapy and became a volunteer clown at a children's hospital after I graduated. I loved it. Introducing a sense of play for both ill children and their worried parents was fun.

I also did hospice work at a local nursing home. While this was not a "fun" activity, I liked listening to the old patients talk about their lives and their concerns. All they really wanted was someone to be with them, to care, to listen. I got a tremendous sense of satisfaction from it because I found that I could be a good listener. I also took some courses in chaplaincy so I felt comfortable responding when they wanted to talk about spiritual or religious matters.

Another satisfying and fun experience was directing the career of an actress—a mother of five who had been housebound for years and whose hobby was performing one-woman plays at home. I was able to book her at various charitable events and finally to perform in a concert hall. Working with a very sensitive, creative woman brought me into the exciting world of theater and taught me the importance of sensitivity when dealing with creative people. It was an incredible experience, which I did for three years. When I left South Bend, Indiana, for Philadelphia, I had the satisfaction of knowing that I had taken her as far as she wanted to go.

But I'm going on and on about myself. Is there anything specific you wanted to know?

Yes! When I was coming in, I overheard your grandchildren rhapsodizing about your 'incredibly delicious, best in the world, chocolate cake.' If you don't mind, could you give me the recipe?

I'm really sorry, but I prefer not to. You see, I think of that cake recipe as part of a family heritage. My grandmother passed it on to my mother and she passed it on to me. I plan to give it to my children. So you can understand why I want to keep it in the family.

I understand. No problem. Now to get on with the interview, do you have any fantasies?

Yes, to be the official taster at a chocolate factory.

What have you learned now that you did not know when you were younger?

Like other women over fifty, I know more now than I did when I was younger. For example, I know it's not always important to be right. And I have learned not to take words personally when someone is in a bad mood.

What is the best advice you remember?

When my children were in school, a lecturer at a parent-teacher session stressed this phrase: "You did the best you could, with what you had, at the time." I tend to be hard on myself when I make mistakes, so I often repeat these words to myself.

What sustains you during difficult times?

Sleep and responsibility. If I don't get enough sleep, or at least some bed rest, I can't function. What gets me out of bed and enables me to do what I have to do is my sense of responsibility to my family. Losing both parents and two younger sisters within six years was very difficult for me.

Does religion play a role in your life?

I see religion and religious traditions as a heritage passed down to me from my parents, grandparents, and great-grandparents. I tried to pass them on to my children and hope they too will pass it on to their children. I love seeing the whole family seated together at the dining room table. I think holidays and observing traditions brings a family closer together.

To get back to the book . . . What did you learn while writing it?

Listening to other women's stories gave me the opportunity to reflect on their lives and my own. I learned that women can endure very difficult circumstances and still retain their zest for living. I learned that in the most painful illnesses, it is possible to retain a sense of control and keep one's sense of humor; that friends are important; that I need to spend more time with creative people; that I need to develop a new interest, perhaps going back to hospice work or volunteering as a "cuddler" in a children's hospital.

What are your hopes for this book?

I hope it sells millions of copies and that I am invited to the Oprah Winfrey show.

What would you like written on your epitaph?

She died, alas, too soon.

If you reach heaven, what would you like God to say to you?

"Welcome. Your grandparents, mother, father, and sisters Finnie and Sheila are waiting to greet you." He might say, "I gave you the gift of life. Did you use it wisely?" To which I would reply, "I tried to the best of my ability."

How would you like to be remembered?

Fondly.

I hope you don't find these questions depressing.

Why should I find questions about death, epitaphs, and how I'd like to be remembered depressing!

Do you have any final last words?

Would you like to buy a copy of my book?

Have you had any feedback on your book?

As it happens, I do have some reviews that I can show you:

"Intellectually stimulating and exquisitely lucid, it nourishes the heart and elevates the spirit to celestial heights. The poetic grace and spiritual insights into the human condition will change your life forever. Filled with inspiring ideas and profound truths, it touches the heart and tickles the funny bone. If I were stranded on a desert island, the one thing I would take with me is mother's book."

—Elise

"In this youth obsessed culture, to read about such remarkably wise and courageous women over the age of fifty is indeed a delight. Each and every one of them fills me with respect and admiration.

I would love to meet any or all of them. Unfortunately, mother won't give me their telephone numbers or addresses."

—Jack

"If you buy a copy of this book we will send you the recipe for Granny's incredibly delicious chocolate cake."

—Alexandra, Justin, Marissa, and Gavin

INTERVIEW WITH YOU

You may find it fun and revealing to interview yourself as I did. I found that thinking about the answers helps us consider aspects of our lives that we take for granted or ignore in the bustle of daily life, and it can spark new possibilities and opportunities that we haven't considered. Here are some questions to ponder:

How do you see yourself—in a word or two?

Tell me something about yourself and what you do.

What do you enjoy? What gives you pleasure? What do you look forward to?

Do you have a fantasy?

What do you know now that you did not know when you were younger?

What advice would you give to others?

What is the best advice you remember?

What sustains you during difficult times?

Does religion play a role in your life?

What would you like written on your epitaph?

How would you like to be remembered?

If you get to heaven, what would you like God to say to you—or you to Him?

PART TWO

PEOPLE WHO CAN HELP US LIVE WELL

THE PSYCHOLOGIST

I've always believed emotional well-being is just as important as physical well-being, so I thought it would be interesting to hear what an experienced psychologist has to say about attaining peace of mind, especially after age fifty. I asked R. Kurt Ebert, Ph.D. for his views:

I treat a wide variety patients who are anxious, depressed, or experience life as dissatisfying or downright miserable. While various drugs have short-term benefit for many, it is my observation that "healing" occurs and symptoms are permanently resolved by our energy within.

It is not what I or any psychologist does or says that makes a real difference. It is what happens within the patient that counts. Whether the problem is emotional or physical, the source our suffering is a manifestation of the energy within us. Our energy alone directs and influences our well-being. We must look within, not without, to find the key to our own destiny.

This view is contrary to both science and religion. Both hold a view that the important determinants of life lie outside ourselves. Those determinants may be the foods we eat, the toxins we ingest, external stresses of life, or the bad genes that we inherit that cause us problems. In the case of religion, All-That-Is, however named, is "out there," in heaven, in nature, or wherever, and we must pray to All-That-Is for grace or mercy or forgiveness in order for All-That-Is to save us from our transgressions, write our name in the Book of Life, or deliver us from evil. The control and power is always outside ourselves.

But what if this view is wrong? What if the key is something that we alone hold and can use to unlock the source of well-being? Our thoughts are a reflection of the energy of our being. Our habitual patterns of thinking disrupt not only the energy of our nervous system, but even more importantly, the energy that influences every aspect of our lives. Stress is nothing more than our habitual reaction to events in the world. It is not something that we find on a street corner or buy in a store.

Recent Nobel Prize-winning research demonstrates that thought and memories have the power to influence genes. Other research has shown that the meridians of acupuncture influence the nervous system, and the relationship of thoughts and nervous system activity to the meridians is a "two-way" street. As it turns out, how and what we think has a profound impact on our well-being. Ultimately, it is the energy from within that heals. One of my favorite sayings is, "If you want to make the world a beautiful place, make your mind a beautiful place." That little saying captures the essence of life.

If what's inside us is at the source of our well-being, what do we need to do to find happiness and contentment and improve our sense of well-being? The first thing that we must do is to let go of the past. One of the great secrets of a happy life, like a good marriage, is a short memory. The past is the graveyard of what was and cannot be changed. Each of us has had many things occur in our lives that we wish had not happened, or we cling to memories of the past as the high points of our existence. We have done things that we regret or feel guilty about. Others have done things that bring up a sense of righteous indignation, and we are unwilling to forgive, which maintains our enmity across years or decades.

As for the things that we have done, there is little reason for guilt unless we deliberately and maliciously set out to harm another. We can regret what has happened as a result of our actions or failures to act, but we should not blame ourselves unless we deliberately intended something bad to happen. We did the best we could, given the way that we were raised and taught to look at the world. As children each of us forms a map of the world and the people in it that guides us unconsciously and limits our actions. What ever happened in the past is over and done. If we do not like what has happened in the past, the only way to overcome it is to let go of it—for it only exists now within us.

In a very similar way, if our past was filled with joys and events that cannot now be re-created for what ever reason, we must let go of these memories and create space for something new. If the past is the highlight of our existence, if the lost things cannot be regained, the future is bleak and can only be viewed with disappointment and despair. After all, what is there to look forward to if all of the good things have already happened and can never be recaptured?

The key to letting go of the past is inside of each of us. To let go of the past, we must forgive ourselves and those that we believe have offended us. Scripturally it is written that, "To err is human and to forgive divine." We must summon up the spark of divine energy that we all possess and let go of our negative thoughts, our sense of shame, blame, fear, and disappointment over the past. When we forgive ourselves or others, the divine energy within us heals, drains the angry, spiteful, vengeful feelings, sooths our pain, and calms our fears. We have been given both the ability to forgive and the ability to use it. It is a matter of exercising our free will and choice. Before any change can be made in our lives, there must be a change in our mind.

It is all a matter of having the right attitude toward life and ourselves. In this sense, a positive attitude is everything.

Letting go of the past also creates space for us to appreciate the present. We live only in the present. The past is gone, and the future is yet to be. Each moment of our existence is a new *now*, a new opportunity to shape what will come into being in the moments that follow. But this is only true if we take the first step of letting go of the past. If the past is allowed to be our "touch stone" for reality, then our understanding requires that we compare "what is" to "what was" before we can understand how to move forward. If we first take a step backward before we can step forward, the best that can happen is that we will wind up in the same place where we started in the first place!

Happiness and joy come from involvement in life, involvement with other people, or in activities that have some meaning for us and contribute positively to our lives and the lives of other people. No matter what the current circumstance of our life, we can find ways to become involved with others—through volunteer work, community activities, religious activities, or strengthening family ties. It can truly be said that joy springs from interaction. Sadness, despair, and misery spring from solitude and isolation. If you cannot find other people to fill your life, get a pet, take walks, and enjoy the beauty of nature. Find a way to become more involved in life.

It is up to us to make our lives work. No one else really knows what makes our hearts sing. At best, other people can only offer us what *they* think is good, or what would make them happy, and by extension think will make us happy. That is probably why each of us has received so many gifts from others that caused us to shake our heads in amazement!

The final step in finding happiness is to make a friend of the creator. The single biggest source of our fear about leaving this world is the fear meeting the creator. Actually, to make a friend of the creator, we must first make friends with ourselves. The two are in actuality one, although we are taught differently. Our religious upbringing teaches most of us to fear the creator, to fear that we have not lived up to the creator's goals and expectations for us. Our failures or "sins," we're taught, will not be received warmly when we "pass through the pearly gates." I believe that this is a mistaken view.

The Judeo-Christian creator is seen as external. We are told that we can meet "him" through a religious encounter, through rituals or prayer and supplication, or through revelation. Many people spend their lives trying to find God, and always look outside themselves. We have been misled. We are looking in the wrong place. God dwells within each of us. We are more than genes and flesh and bones. Genes, flesh, and bones do not have the divine spark of life that each of us possesses. They are what are left when we have gone. We all have the spirit of God within us and we need to bring that spirit out. Yet we bury our spirit under our guilt, our shame, and our fears. We separate ourselves from our own spirituality by believing that we are unworthy, that we are "sinners" who will be cast out if found out.

In my perspective, the creator is really like a loving parent who points out what should be done but never scolds us when we fail to listen. We are allowed to make our own mistakes and learn our own lessons, in our time. Those of us brought up in the Judeo-Christian tradition know of the Ten Commandments. We have learned to judge our actions and the actions of others in terms of the "dos" and "don'ts" of the Commandments. We learned to think in terms of "sins", and fear that our transgressions will be held against us.

I offer a different interpretation of the Ten Commandments than is traditionally taught. In my mind, the Ten Commandments were given to man as an act of mercy by a loving creator who wishes our lives to be full, happy, and filled with well-being. The Ten Commandments are not demands, but rather directions or instructions for how we can achieve well-being. They are good rules for living life. If everyone followed them all of the time, who could argue that life would not be better?

I began to view the Ten Commandments as an act of mercy accidentally—if there is such a thing as an accident. I happened to be looking up the word "mercy" in a dictionary when I came across a reference to the "mercy seat." I had never heard of the "mercy seat" and took note of the reference, which led me to the Bible. The instructions for creating the "mercy seat" are found in the Bible just after the instructions on building the Arc of the Covenant in which the tablets containing the Ten Commandments were to be placed. The "mercy seat" was to be placed on top of the Arc and was a place from which the creator could sit and commune with the Israelites.

It struck me that placing the "mercy seat" above the Ten Commandments was not an accident. It also struck me that the Bible mentions no penalties for breaking the Commandments. The Commandments are things that we are advised to do or not to do, not things that we will be penalized for by the creator if we do not heed them. Violating the Commandments will not bring the creator's wrath, but violating them will bring a lack of well-being in our lives. The creator was simply admonishing us, as any parent would, to "watch out for strangers," "not run into the street," or "not touch a hot stove."

We alone judge ourselves. The creator does not judge us. Unlike the creator depicted by our religious heritage as a vengeful, punitive being to be feared, the creator promotes life in every form. Look around, life abounds in every conceivable nook and cranny of the world. After all is said and done, "Love Story" had it right: Love is all about "not having to say you're sorry."

YOUR THOUGHTS:

_____

_____

_____

_____

_____

_____

THE PHYSICIAN

I like my doctor because she has good common sense, and I have confidence in her—which is a good thing because the healing relationship between patient and physician plays a vital role in medical care. Studies indicate that people who like their physicians and communicate well with them, get better care and better results. Here is some healthcare guidance for women over fifty from Donna Shore, MSc, M.D, CCFP :

Now that the average life expectancy for women is over eighty, we can expect to spend one-third of our lives after menopause. We face different hormonal and age-related health issues than we did during our childbearing years. The health needs of women over fifty necessitate regular doctor visits, annually or at least biannually, for primary medical care. The focus should be on health maintenance and disease prevention. This care should include a physical examination and laboratory investigations, both guided by the appropriate age and life-cycle issues.

A woman's relationship with a healthcare professional will be most fruitful if she has established a relationship with someone with whom she feels comfortable and can communicate easily. This should not be a family member or friend who may not necessarily be at ease to discuss sensitive or personal topics.

In North America, the average age of menopause (defined as the cessation of menses for a period of twelve month) is fifty-one, plus or minus two years. But it rarely occurs without some forewarning. The "perimenopause" period is the time leading up to menopause. The primary health concerns that emerge during perimenopause and persist beyond it are the increasing risk of cardiovascular disease, such as heart attacks, angina, and high cholesterol, as well as osteoporosis (the thinning and /or fractured bones that produces the stooped-like posture we often see in older people, especially women). The risk of osteoporosis is a very high rate of hip fractures, which may result in hospitalization and often death.

Whether you see a primary care physician (family doctor), gynecologist, or other specialist, it's wise to prepare before your appointment. Write down concerns and questions in decreasing order of priority and address them in that order. Be prepared to schedule a return visit if you have many questions. Ask for written materials: pamphlets or handouts to reinforce and remind you of any recommendations made.

To make the most of a medical appointment, here are some suggestions:

- Investigate your family history. A positive family history refers to the occurrence of any disease in close relatives such as mother, father, or siblings. The younger age the disease appears and the more frequently, the more significance it has to you and your physician. A pattern of a particular illness that has occurred repeatedly in more distant family members may be of consequence as well. A positive family history of osteoporosis or early heart disease would necessitate a more aggressive approach to detection and management of these disorders, for example.

- Estimate your dietary intake of calcium, vitamin D, and fat to ensure you are meeting recommended levels for calcium and vitamin D and not exceeding recommended levels for fat. Discuss with your doctor your optimal need of these nutrients and how you may reach these levels.
- Exercise—especially the weight-bearing type like walking and cycling—is crucial for bone strength. Physical activity keeps heart disease risk low. Discuss with your doctor which activities are best for you and at what level you should begin if you are not yet active.
- Natural products, herbs, and supplements may have an impact on your health and can potentially interact with other medications or substances that you may be taking. Make sure your doctor is aware of all the products you consume.
- Hormone replacement therapy (HRT), like any other medical treatment, has both risks and benefits associated with it. Recent evidence from the Women's' Health Initiative Study has recommended against HRT as a low risk preventative treatment for women, but HRT may still be appropriate for selected women for management of particularly difficult problems.
- Routine gynecological exams should continue throughout a women's life. Ask your healthcare professional if you still require a Pap test, and don't neglect to report any bleeding that occurs after the menopause has been completed; it may be a sign of a potential problem. Mammograms have definitely proved able to detect breast cancer before disease is evident. The exact interval of screening recommendations varies. Ask your doctor which applies to you.

Continue to take responsibility for your health. Ask questions and be an active partner with your doctor to keep yourself as healthy as you could be! Be knowledgeable but be skeptical about any consumer website. Many websites offer medical information; some are not as reliable as others. Ask your doctor before following any medical advice from a website.

YOUR THOUGHTS:

_____

_____

_____

_____

_____

_____

THE SEX THERAPIST

For many women over fifty, the subject of sex seems awkward or uncomfortable. Some women assume that sexual relations wane with age or after years of marriage to the same man. Other women—single, divorced, or widowed—may find themselves in new relationships where expectations about sex have changed significantly since they were in their twenties or thirties. For all women over fifty, I thought that a sex therapist could shed light on these concerns, so I interviewed Kimberly Flemke, Ph.D., of the Institute for Sex Therapy, and Assistant Professor at Drexel University's Couples & Family Therapy Program:

Within my clinical practice, I see many women in their fifties and older, some for individual therapy and others for couples and sex therapy. Low sexual desire is one of the most common issues that these women face. This issue can often generate feelings of guilt and shame. Women with low sexual desire also tend to develop feelings of resentment towards partners who have higher levels of sexual desire, in response to feeling pressure to have more sex.

I suggest various products (from topical creams to toys) to aid these women. The most common product I recommend for improving both arousal and sexual satisfaction is Zestra, an oil that is rubbed all over a women's vulva, including her clitoris. As it is rubbed in, it will heat up and tingle, generally enhancing a woman's orgasm and sexual satisfaction. This product has been clinically tested with positive results and can be bought at drug stores as well as purchased online.

I also suggest that women consider trying vibrators, especially for those who have never had an orgasm. Vibrators can be purchased online at many reputable websites, including: **www.amazon.com** (under "sex and sexuality" or just searching for "vibrator"), **www.sinclair.com**, and **www.adameve. com**. These products are mailed discreetly, which usually helps alleviate anxiety about the purchase. Many women report feeling "naughty" or "dirty," but my experience is that many fifty-plus women are quite surprised to learn how widely used and socially accepted vibrators are today by women of all ages. Many women are also surprised to learn that vibrators are not just for individual pleasure, but can be used with partners to create excitement in the bedroom.

Other highly effective vibrators are handheld back massagers, which can be found at a store like Brookstone. A handheld massager popular among women is Hitachi's, "The Wand," which can be purchased with vibrator attachments. When buying these items, I usually tell women to try out different kinds to see what they finds most pleasing. Many women report enjoying the very small vibrators, such as the "silver bullet," "pulsing orbiter," and the "pocket rocket," which are battery operated.

Through buying these toys, many women are surprised to discover that it's through clitoral stimulation that will cause an orgasm, not the actual thrusting of something inside the vagina (unless it's stimulating the g-spot).

Low sexual desire is particularly relevant for women over fifty for a few reasons. First, the primary message given to women in our culture is that *only* young, beautiful women in their twenties and thirties, with firm breasts and tight bodies, are sexy and, therefore, sexual. Addressing how these messages have become internalized and "bought into" is important for women throughout their lifespan, but especially for women over fifty. Many women do not realize that their "lack of desire" may be linked to having those messages define their own sexual identity. If they see themselves outside the narrowly defined Hollywood definition of "sexual," many women unknowingly accept and conform to these non-sexual expectations.

Since desire is actually something that takes place within the mind, it is able to occur at *any* age. It requires women to give themselves *permission* to want sexual pleasure because they believe that they *deserve* sexual pleasure. Desire is simply positive anticipation of wanting sexual satisfaction. By rejecting Hollywood's implicit messages to women over fifty, and *choosing* sexual desire, women can put themselves back in the driver's seat of their own sexuality.

The experience of menopause also creates sexual issues, as women's bodies are completely changing physically and hormonally. Often women will complain of vaginal dryness that can create painful intercourse. I suggest that women first have a physical exam to make sure there are no medical issues, such as vulvodynia or vestibulitis, requiring medical treatment. For vaginal dryness, however, I recommend using a lubricant supplement, such as KY jelly, which can be purchased at any pharmacy, commonly located near the condoms and other forms of birth control.

Another common issue is being divorced and not knowing how to date in today's social scene. Because many women have not dated since before they were married, perhaps twenty to thirty years ago, there is no certainty about current dating rules, sexual expectations, and where to meet people to date.

A case example involves a woman I was seeing in her mid-fifties, Claire (whose name has been changed to protect her anonymity). She had divorced her husband of twenty-three years the previous year. Claire wanted to attempt dating again, but did not know where to start. She was quite distressed over not having met anyone to date since her divorce.

I asked Claire, "Is your cab light on, or is your cab light off?" My question challenged Claire to evaluate honestly whether she was sending signals that she is single and available or driving by people signaling that she's "off duty." She laughed and admitted that her light was probably off more than she realized because she was really scared of dating again.

We brainstormed some ideas about where she could meet men her age who would feel safe and put her at ease. Since Claire's job was located in an urban area, we discussed possibly going to a "happy hour" after work with some friends. Happy hours often provide an informal, non-threatening environment of working professionals who are seeking to unwind and mingle after a long day. She took my advice, asked some friends to accompany her, and discovered she enjoyed herself very much. She was surprised to see other colleagues, who introduced her to their friends. Her social networking experience became quite positive, as she began talking with people she had never met before. She even wound up exchanging business cards with two different men.

At our next session, Claire was stressed over her new dating prospects, one of whom had called her already. Claire didn't know what the expectations were for going on a date in today's world. Her first questions were, "Should I expect him to pay or should I offer? Or should we split the bill?" I explained that this can be negotiated with her date. Many people feel that the person who calls to ask the other out on a date usually picks up the tab. Other people are more comfortable splitting costs and feel less pressure for later expectations. Since women often ask men out in today's world, the rules are far less rigid than in the past. Everything is open for discussion.

She casually joked and said, "Well, since I had my hysterectomy five years ago, I guess I don't have to worry about carrying around my diaphragm like the old days." My immediate response took her by surprise. I emphatically explained that it was imperative that she uses a condom with any man she sleeps with. I explained the greater concern is the extremely high prevalence of sexually transmitted diseases, particularly Herpes and HPV (which can lead to cervical cancer in women). I suggested that she be prepared and carry her own condoms, in case the male was not carrying his own. I also explained that she should not consider having sex with anyone who was not willing to wear one because she could be putting her own life at risk. Finally, I told Claire that even if someone comes prepared to wear a condom, she should reject any pressure to have sex until she decides she's ready, no matter how long they've been dating. She sighed in relief and agreed.

I suggested another dating venue, online dating, which has grown exponentially over the past few years. She hesitated at first, not feeling "computer savvy" enough to consider it a possibility. I explained that online dating can be a safe way to dip your toe in the dating scene because it allows you to check things out before plunging in. For example, you can turn on your computer and just see who's out there. You can talk online as a way to decide if you even want to meet in person. It also gives you the ability to determine how much information you are comfortable sharing about yourself at your own pace. Online dating allows people to be selective without fearing this is the only date you may ever have again. I encouraged her to consider viewing popular online sites without joining (such as Match.com, Yahoo.personals, and Eharmony).

I reminded her that she should never disclose any personal information that could leave her vulnerable (ie: financial status, social security number, address, etc.). I also encourage women to wait a while before giving out their home or cell phone numbers in case, after getting to know someone online, they might regret having this person be able to call them. I told her that, should she ever decide to meet someone in person, it should be in a public place (ie: restaurant, bar, café) and that she take herself to and from so that she's both safe and has the ability to leave at any point. It's also a good idea to let someone know the location of where she'll be and approximately when she expects to return, so that her whereabouts are known. Lastly, having a cell phone with her is a must.

The following week Claire bounced into my office and reported that she was in disbelief at the hundreds of prospective dating partners within a short mile radius. She told me that after viewing the numerous websites for three nights and reading the many interesting biographies and seeing their pictures, she decided to finally join one. She explained that she was having fun just emailing different people whom she seemed to share common interests. She was amazed at the overwhelming responses she was receiving. More importantly, Claire was feeling a renewed sense of confidence that she could figure out how to date again. She left my office and informed me that she's finally ready to turn on her cab light; however, she sheepishly confessed that her new problem will be figuring out how to squeeze in all her expected dates!

YOUR THOUGHTS:

_____

_____

_____

_____

_____

_____

THE DENTIST

I sometimes hear people say, "Had I to do it over again, I would have taken better care of my teeth." We all know that we need to brush and floss, but not everyone is aware of other options, such as the advantages of braces at an older age, or why it's sometimes a good investment to put money into expensive dental work. Here are some basic facts from Gary H. Katz, D.D.S., F.A.G.D., who has been a dentist for over thirty years and has many patients over age fifty:

To prevent dental problems, I give patients this basic advice:

- See your dentist on a regular basis for a thorough examination and a cleaning. This may be two, three, or even four times a year if you have gum problems. During this examination the dentist checks for tumors, infections, cavities, gum disease, and other abnormalities that may be present. X-rays are taken periodically to show hidden problems. Prevention is the most efficient way of spending your dental dollars.
- Brush for two minutes in the morning and before retiring. Thoroughly floss at night. Clean your tongue with a special scraper.
- Don't commit dental suicide by sucking on candy or drinking sweetened beverages all day long, which will cause rampant decay over a short time. Decay-causing

bacteria convert sugar into acid and remain active for thirty minutes after the sugar is gone. The result is acid bathing the teeth constantly. Some patients develop this habit because of dry mouth caused by various medications. Carry a water bottle with you to keep the mouth moist instead.

People don't like to talk about bad breath, but it has several causes that should be understood if it's to be corrected: Periodontal (gum) disease is a frequent cause of severe mouth odor in the senior population when pus pockets from infection form around the teeth. This condition is dangerous and requires dental treatment. The infection can cause problems in other parts of the body. Dry mouth, anti-anxiety medications and radiation treatments of the head and neck are other common causes of bad breath.

Bad breath can also result from food such as garlic, which may persist for twenty-four hours after eating. Mouth rinses, combined with cleaning the tongue, can help. Systemic causes (stomach distress, diabetes, and other illnesses) can also cause bad breath.

A study commissioned by plastic surgeons found that the smile is considered the most important feature of the face. Advances in cosmetic dentistry techniques can restore beautiful smiles. These techniques include:

Tooth lightening or bleaching is a simple solution for dark or stained teeth. Teeth are treated with an oxidizing agent in the dentist's office, followed by home treatments using custom made trays. Teeth can be lightened eight to ten shades. Bleaching works best on yellow and brown stains but less so on gray and bluish colors. Over-the-counter products are less effective and are unsupervised. Bleaching will only lighten natural tooth structure and not man-made dental work.

Porcelain veneers are recommended for teeth that are chipped, heavily filled, crooked, or greatly discolored-

Capping is recommended for teeth with inadequate structure and can be restored with veneers. Modern advances and new materials fabricate all porcelain caps on front teeth, eliminating the previously used metal substrate that caused dark lines around the gums.

Orthodontics (braces), once thought to be for only the young, are quite successful in adults over fifty. Implants are the latest state-of-the-art method to replace missing teeth. Titanium cylinders are embedded in the bone as a permanent artificial roots to support caps. The implant integrates with the jawbone and feels like a natural tooth. Multiple teeth or even an entire mouth can be restored to eliminate the need for removable partial and full dentures. (No need to take teeth out at night. Patients who wear full dentures lose 65 percent of their chewing function. Since dentures are held in by suction, they often loosen at embarrassing moments. Dentures also contribute to loss of jawbone over the years.)

"If only I were younger, I would spend the money for the dental treatments" is a comment I hear all too often from every age group over fifty. My response is: "How long are you going to live?" Since no one really knows, a quality of life issue is based on your value system. What is it worth to be able to smile proudly, chew all foods properly (especially the healthy fibrous ones), speak properly, be pain free, and feel secure that your teeth stay in?

Good dental care is more than cosmetic, however. Scientists have recently discovered correlations between gum disease (periodontitis) and heart disease, premature births, and uncontrolled diabetes. I encourage my patients to do what it takes to have a healthy mouth and be on a regular prevention regimen. As long as you are physically able, have the necessary dental problems corrected. As we age, there may be a time when ill health will prevent major treatment. I was once called to a nursing home to help a patient who had rotted teeth and an old, ill-fitting denture. She could no longer chew, and dental infection was affecting the rest of her body. Unfortunately there was little we could do to help. It's a heart-breaking situation to see. Don't let that happen to you or a loved one. Remember, be true to your teeth or they'll be false to you.

YOUR THOUGHTS:

_____

_____

_____

_____

_____

_____

THE OPHTHALMOLOGIST

At one time my friends were concerned with the most flattering shade of eye shadow. Now their concerns are good vision, dry, gritty eyes, and, in some cases, glaucoma. I thought it important to hear what an ophthalmologist has to say about proper eye care. At the same time, I learned a few things about how to communicate better with an ophthalmologist or, for that matter, any medical specialist. Here is what Dr. Peter G. Gross, M.D., Ph.D., has to say:

Glaucoma is one of the most prevalent eye conditions of people over fifty. For most people, glaucoma has no symptoms until it is too late. Although it is potentially blinding, it is preventable and controllable with regular visits to the ophthalmologist. An appropriate and practical frequency of eye checkups for perfectly healthy eyes would be every two years after age fifty and every year after age sixty-five. If you have a family history of glaucoma, this frequency of visits should be doubled even if your eyes are healthy. If glaucoma is suspected at any time, a baseline glaucoma workup should be carried out with appropriate diligence.

Well-informed patients will take good care of themselves. It is therefore important to develop a good working relationship with your doctor. Be sure to understand your doctor's instructions and exact concerns. Be sure to give your doctor feedback about your own concerns regarding glaucoma or any other eye condition, its treatment, and clinical follow-up.

Stay informed by reading on your own and searching the Internet. But be sure to treat your ophthalmologist with kindness and respect, and do not simply challenge your doctor with some information you have uncovered on your own. Remember, there is no one who cares more about your eyes than your ophthalmologist, even if he or she does not verbalize it. The last thing you want to do is question the doctor's judgment and dedication in a way that will be detrimental to your working relationship. (Just recall how you felt when your children compared you with someone else's parents. So do ask for information and explanations, but do not challenge the doctor's judgment; instead, ask more questions that will resolve any nagging issues on your mind.)

If your concerns are still not satisfied, then just explain your concern as clearly as you can and listen to your doctor's response. Remember, a doctor just like yours wrote what you read elsewhere without having your specific situation as a focus of attention. If your concerns still remain unsatisfied, ask your doctor whether you should get a second opinion and where. You are much better to follow your doctor's choice of a second opinion than your own choice or a friend's choice. After all, if you do not trust your doctor's integrity (as distinct from his or her knowledge and skills), then why were you consulting him or her in the first place?

Macular degeneration is another age-related eye condition. Much high-tech progress is taking place in the fight to control this condition. Consulting your ophthalmologist is the best way to keep up to date with the latest developments. The most effective precautionary measures consist of daily checking the vision of each eye one at a time for about one second each, appropriate vitamin supplements (eye vitamins are a good starting point) without overdosing in any one vitamin or mineral, and wearing sunglasses in bright light. In general body terms, the best thing one can do for preserving the macula is to optimize one's cardiovascular fitness.

Floaters are normal development of aging, just like wrinkles and gray hair. The vitreous (the transparent gel in the eyeball) is a marvel of perfection in our youth, but it gradually degrades over time from the shaking it receives every time we take a step, move our heads, and blink an eye. Eventually, the vitreous separates from the retina and the vitreous fibers of collagen then move around, casting moving shadows on the retina that are perceived as floaters of various shapes. Any sudden change in floaters must trigger an eye exam no later than the next day, the most common concern being a tear or detachment of the far peripheral retina.

Eyelid care is especially important as we age, although we may take them for granted. The eyelid protects the front of the eye and its functions are virtually countless. Eyelid care requires the following no-nos: no eye rubbing; no eye touching; and no eyelid squeezing. Violations of any of these no-nos increase the rate of destruction of the fine elastic fibers and suspension ligaments that keep the eyelids in perfect position and hasten the development of baggy eyes and droopy eyelids, which will occur soon enough anyway as the orbital fat undergoes atrophy with increasing age. Most itchy feelings are self-limited and disappear within five to fifteen seconds. Try to resist rubbing or scratching your eyelids. If the itchy feelings do not go away, then wash your hands and rinse around the closed eyelids with plenty of clean water. If they still itch after that, an ophthalmologist should be consulted.

The blinking action of the eyelids is so very important and requires special attention. At every blink, the gliding action of the eyelid over the cornea re-establishes the integrity of the tear film. A good quality tear film is necessary for clear vision. When people read, watch television, watch the computer screen, or are intent on looking at anything, there is a tendency to blink less. This causes both degradation in the quality of the vision as well as a drying of the cornea.

When the cornea becomes dry it hurts and becomes damaged, usually on a microscopic scale not visible to the naked eye. The signs of this type of damage from drying are a sensation of grittiness, like sand in the eye. If not properly heeded and taken care of with lubricating eye drops, it can worsen until it feels like there is a foreign agent in the eye. Consulting an ophthalmologist is important because allowing the process to continue unchecked can lead to significant breakdown of the cornea and eventually an infection (called corneal ulcer) that can, in its most severe state, lead to the loss of the eye. So blinking is important both in the tear-wetting process and vision process. Good blinking action requires healthy eyelids as well as good general health. There are many illnesses that interfere with good blinking function and it is important to seek medical help in all such cases.

Computer Vision Syndrome (CVS) affects most people who spend more than three hours a day at the computer. Symptoms include tired or dry eyes, blurry or double vision, headaches, and stiff neck. The more time you spend at the computer, the more these symptoms will be accelerated.

To overcome these problems, wear glasses with anti-glare coating, look away from the screen often, and focus for ten to fifteen seconds on a distant object. Every thirty minutes, blink a few times and close your eyes. If you use a desk lamp, place it to the side of your computer screen and make sure the light is no brighter than your monitor. Increase the text size for reading comfort by hitting the "view" button at the top of your screen. Talk to your doctor about taking vitamins and supplements that help protect your vision. If your symptoms do not improve, check with your ophthalmologist.

Your eyes are more precious than any jewel. Guard them carefully. Visit an ophthalmologist for routine checkups every two years even if there is nothing wrong and every year after age sixty-five.

YOUR THOUGHTS:

_____
_____
_____
_____
_____
_____

THE OSTEOPATH

Back pain can be excruciating. After moving the wrong way and being laid up in bed for two days, I promised myself that when I got better I would find out what I could do to prevent back problems in the future—and I did. Because back problems effect so many of us, I asked Alexander S. Nicholas, D.O., F.A.A.O., chairman of the Department of Osteopathic Manipulative Medicine of the Philadelphia College of Osteopathic Medicine, to share his knowledge of back problems, their prevention, and treatment.

Over 80 percent of adults will have at least one episode of acute, low back pain that requires them to seek medical attention. Musculoskeletal problems are one of the most prevalent reasons for doctor visits. Billions of dollars are spent worldwide on medical and surgical treatments for musculoskeletal problems. They may involve pain, stiffness, difficulty walking, trouble sleeping, and work disability. The inability to drive, sit, or enjoy normal sexual relations, as well as other concerns, such as caring for children or grandchildren, may all be related to problems in the musculoskeletal system.

Conditions such as osteoarthritis and osteoporosis are in the forefront of the musculoskeletal management of the pre- and post-menopausal patient. Other common conditions, such as strains and sprains, may be more common. Another 'fifty-plus' condition is degenerative disc disease secondary to dehydration of the intervertebral disc, which decreases the cushioning effect between the vertebrae. This can increase stress on the spinal joint and the vertebral ligaments, resulting in instability of the spine. It can also cause pain and loss of motion.

Osteopathic manipulation may be able to improve loss of motion and the pain associated with it. Various techniques, such as adding small springing forces and stretching of the tissues, may be helpful. The physician must take into account the nature of the problem and other medical history and determine which applicable technique is best for each individual. Other treatment modalities may be helpful in the care of your back problem, such as over-the-counter non-steroidal anti-inflammatory medications, analgesics, muscle relaxants, and anti-depressants to help with chronic pain, poor sleep patterns, and depression associated with pain.

One of the most important things the women over age fifty can do is to *prevent* problems of the musculoskeletal system. That means appropriate, regular exercise. The important word here is *regular*. Too many times the "weekend warrior" mentality causes patients to strain and sprain their muscles and ligaments. Exercise needs to be suitable for the individual. A non-symptomatic person training for the Olympics differs from a fifty-plus patient exercising for health. Many people need medical care after lifting weights, doing yoga and Pilates, and aerobics that they aren't adequately prepared to do, have overdone, or have done incorrectly.

One of the most common injuries that brings patients into the doctor's office is the strain or sprain secondary to stretching exercises. You must not stretch when the muscles are "cold." You should first try walking or gently going through the motions of a planned exercise before a stretching routine. A warm shower or hot packs before stretching can also help limit stretching injuries and prevent new ones.

When stretching, you should not stretch to pain! Stretch only to a comfortable tension for fifteen to twenty seconds and repeat carefully three to five times. Using isometric contractions of the stretched muscle can also be helpful during the stretch.

If you ever feel that you have strained your back, neck, leg, etc., apply ice packs for twenty minutes and repeat every three to four hours. If you are just stiff and achy, moist heat for fifteen to twenty minutes every three to four hours is appropriate. If you feel a little more pain than just an ache and think you may have done too much physically, moist heat followed by ice packs in the previous described time limits is also helpful.

When considering back pain and its prevention, think for a moment about all you do on a daily basis. Like most women, you make the bed; bend to wash your legs and feet; dry your hair and your feet; bend over the sink to wash your face; bend and lift packages from the back seat or trunk of a car; bend to put dishes in the dishwasher and laundry in and out of the washing machine and dryer; lift heavy dishes or pots in and out of the oven; clip your toenails; vacuum; and last but not least, have sex. A number of my patients have had acute back pain from over arching during sexual activity. Bending in the garden, raking leaves; shoveling snow; pushing up a stuck window; and walking the dog are other common ways women hurt themselves and cause them to seek medical care.

Education is the best way to limit mechanical musculoskeletal pains. The best way I know to prevent many activities from causing problems is to teach my patients to remember and follow this rule: *Never let your nose go in front of your toes and never, ever turn your nose away from your toes when you are in the process of lifting or just straightening!*

This means that anytime you bend forward, if your chest and head are in front of your pelvis, you're looking for trouble. If you find yourself in this position, which is not unusual, don't turn your trunk to the side away from the direction your feet are pointing because, if you straighten up from that position, it can cause the weight of your upper body to be affected by lever actions, thus generating hundreds of pounds per square inch. So watch out when lifting bags of potting soil, laundry baskets, grocery bags, potted plants, as well as baby and toddler grandchildren.

Getting in and out of a car is another common cause of back problems. To prevent them, I advise my patients to pretend they are ninety years old and need to protect their backs. When getting into a car, open the door and turn so your back is toward the seat and your hand is behind you on the seat. Slowly lower yourself down onto the seat. With both hands behind you, knuckles bent, push your rear end towards the back of the seat and slide yourself forward, one leg at a time. To exit the car, open the door, swing the outside leg out and follow with the inside leg. You should now be sitting, facing the open door. Holding on to the steering wheel, or to the door, slowly lift yourself up and out.

If a patient has a back problem, it is always best to start at your physician's office. Not everyone is clear about the difference between a chiropractor and an osteopath. Chiropractors are non-physician lay practitioners who are trained in manipulation of the spine. They are not licensed to prescribe medication, perform medical treatment such as surgery. They are solely manipulative in their education. Osteopathic physicians are physicians and are licensed to practice all forms of medicine. They are taught the principles of osteopathy and osteopathic manipulative treatment even though there is a specialty branch that focuses on neuromusculoskeletal medicine.

YOUR THOUGHTS:

THE DERMATOLOGIST

A little sign on my dermatologist's desk reads, "Wrinkled is not what I wanted to be when I grew up." That seems to be a good reason why skin care is important. Skin cancer prevention and maintaining healthy looking skin are the domain of the dermatologist. That seems obvious, but I know many women who get skin care advice only from beauticians. I asked Karen K. Deasey, M.D., of Main Line Health System's Division of Dermatology at Bryn Mawr Hospital, to discuss skin care for women over fifty:

It is never too late to try to rejuvenate your skin. While we cannot turn back the clock, many things can be done as part of a sensible skin care program to refine your skin and minimize wrinkles and the signs of aging. Sensible skin care does not have to be expensive or complicated. Less is more, and pricey does not mean more effective. Consistency is important. Use products that you like and that are compatible with your skin. When you read the word "cosmeceutical" on a product, it refers to cosmetics that have therapeutic value and do not require a prescription.

Wrinkles are not caused by lack of moisturizer, although dry skin can accentuate wrinkles. Wrinkles are caused by genetics (Look at your parents' faces and compare yours.), gravity, smoking, sleep lines, expression, and sun exposure. The only factors you can really control are smoking and sun exposure. But using a facial moisturizer can help to de-emphasize wrinkles that are accentuated by dry skin and protect against sun damage. Use a facial moisturizer every morning, whether cloudy in July or sunny in December, with an SPF (sun protection factor) of 15 or higher. Suggestions include products from Eucerin, Olay, L'Oreal, Neutrogena, Ponds, various cosmetic lines, and specific products such as Cetaphil Facial Moisturizer SPF 15, DML Face cream, and products sold in physician's offices. These products are referred to as "day moisturizers", facial sunscreens, and facial moisturizer with SPF. They are usually not waterproof, are formulated for delicate facial skin, and make a base for foundation and makeup. They are usually applied over any other morning anti-aging products you might be using. Obviously, don't smoke.

Age can be given away by not only facial skin, but also by your neck and hands, so treat your neck and hands as you do your face. Many baby-boomers and most senior citizens did not use sunscreens during the critical sun exposure years—from age one to eighteen. Thus, the search for the fountain of youth!

Cleansers—Plain water can be an appropriate cleanser for some people. Facial and regular soaps are also fine if you have oily or acne-prone skin. For sensitive and easily irritated facial skin, Cetaphil or Aquanil cleanser are best. Many doctor's office products and salon lines have excellent cleansers. A cleansing at night and a warm or cool water rinse each morning is easy and quick.

Alpha-hydroxys—Products with alpha-hydroxy acids have been available for over ten years. They are applied as night creams and are the basis of the "lunchtime peels" so popular in the recent past. Topical creams include Alpha Hydrox, Avon's Anew line, Aquaglycolic products, salon/spa products, and doctor's office products such as Glycolix, Murad, Physicians Choice, Jan Marini, Neostrata, and numerous other lines, all variations on a theme. They are usually applied as a night cream. Alpha-hydroxy acids can texturize, clarify, smooth, and brighten "muddy" mottled, lifeless middle age skin. They may even help lessen pore size, although this is questionable. With consistent use, facial skin will begin to appear more youthful after perhaps four to six weeks. That "maidenly blush" and "girlish glow" will start to return. Alpha-hydroxy acids will peel and exfoliate without visible effects of flaking and irritation. There are also alpha-hydroxy containing washes, cleansers, astringents, and toners.

Antioxidants help repair photodamage (sun damage), fine wrinkling, and possibly capillary damage, which leads to redness and broken blood vessels on the cheeks, forehead, and chin. The best-known antioxidants are vitamin C and green tea. Products include Citrix Face Cream, the Cellex C line, Lancôme's Vitabolic, and various green tea containing products such as Replenix Cream and Serum. Antioxidants tend to be among the more expensive of the topical anti-aging products, but with repeated use, skin will be firmer, smoother and more supple, and fine wrinkles will be less obvious.

Retin A, Renova and tretinoin (generic) are topical vitamin acids, one of the original anti-aging concepts. They require a prescription, are used for sun damage, age spots, and fine wrinkles, and are applied nightly or less frequently, as tolerated. They often cause dryness, flaking, and mild irritation. "Retinoids" are used in conjunction with other topical anti-aging products. Most prescription plans don't cover "Retin-A", and it can be expensive.

Bland moisturizers are applied when facial skin is sensitive, irritated, or dry by themselves or with any of the anti-aging products. Suggestions include Cetaphil Moisture Cream and DML lotion. These can be used head to toe and are also great for eczema and "dry skin" anywhere on the body. These can be purchased at a pharmacy or a physician's office.

Start with one product at a time, adding a new product every week or two. If irritation or an adverse effect occurs, you can then usually identify the causative product. Cleanse the face at night. Then apply the alpha-hydroxy and/or the green tea antioxidant. Rinse or cleanse the face in the morning and then apply the vitamin C and/or the green tea. Finish with a day moisturizer, and age appropriate makeup. Remember that a bland moisturizer can be applied as the first layer. Also note that product lines can be mixed and matched.

Fillers and Botox—There are several injectable agents that can be used to fill facial lines or paralyze facial muscles. The "gold standard" injectable filler is Zyderm/Zyplast (bovine or cow collagen) that has a tried and true safety record. Newer fillers such as Cosmodern/Cosmoplast (human collagen), and hyaluronic acid (Restylane products and Hyalaform products) are also safe and effective. Unfortunately, these products are not permanent, are expensive, and are not covered by health insurance plans. Medical grade silicone is still used, but can lump and can sometimes migrate. With all the fillers, there is some discomfort on injection, and the possibility of bruising and swelling. Botox (botulinis toxin) is injected in minute amounts to paralyze facial muscles around the eyes, forehead, and lips. It is also not permanent, and is expensive. Any of these injectables can be repeated at three to six month intervals. Duration of response varies according to location and facial expression activity.

Plastic surgery—This includes face lifts, eye lifts (blepharoplasty) and various "tucks and lifts". The choice of a more aggressive approach is up to the individual. Consultation with an accomplished plastic or oculoplastic surgeon should be sought on the basis of skill, reputation, and results with other patients.

Hair—By the early forties, many women will notice recession of their hair line, with some thinning at the crown of the scalp. The degree of loss is often genetic, and the terms female pattern hair loss and *androgenetic alopecia* are used to describe the condition. Many women notice finer hair texture in middle age, and that their hair does not seem to grow as fast or as long as it once did. "See through heads" are almost always inherited, and if pedigrees are examined or old pictures observed, all the women in a family will be noticeably thinned, thus the term "see through head." Treatments for female pattern loss include topical Rogaine (minoxidil) that is applied once or twice daily, and Propecia (finasteride) taken orally as a pill. Propecia, a prescription drug, is not FDA approved for use in women, so this is "off label" use. It is not to be used in premenopausal women, as it can cause birth defects in a developing fetus. These medications can slow and stop hair loss, and may stimulate new growth.

Sun protection—It is important to protect all the skin from the ravages of the sun's rays (ultraviolet A and B). Consistent use of sunscreen with an SPF of 15 to 30 can protect against skin cancers (basal cell cancer, squamous cell cancer, and melanoma), and can prevent dermatoheliosis (the "old bag" look with wrinkles, folds, creases, mottling and a perpetual tan). Ideally this protection should start in early childhood. But it is never too late to start!

Don't be discouraged. Be consistent. Use good products. And be patient. While you can't go back to looking like you did when you were nineteen, thirty-nine is not bad!

YOUR THOUGHTS:

_____

_____

_____

_____

_____

_____

THE PHARMACIST

With so many of us taking different medicines, and physicians not always having the time to answer questions, it makes sense to have a pharmacist with whom we can communicate. Many health insurance providers are encouraging patients to fill prescriptions through mail order services, but after listening to Helen, a registered pharmacist, I realize that a good neighborhood pharmacist can be a critical partner in our medical care.

I have been a pharmacist for twenty-eight years. I work at a small independent drugstore and am on first name basis with most of our customers. I know their ailments and am familiar with the medicines they are taking. They trust me to give them good advice, and I take the time to be thorough when I answer their questions.

It is important to choose a pharmacist who will take the time to listen to you. Equally important, buy all your medications at the same pharmacy. If you go to different doctors, you may be given medications that interact with each other. If they do, the pharmacist will phone your doctor or tell you and not fill the prescription. A pharmacist can also give advice about medicines, such as not to take aspirin with a specific drug.

If you are taking a particular medication, it can be helpful to take certain vitamins or minerals with it. For example, you are on an antibiotic, it can provoke a yeast infection, so taking vitamin B is recommended. If you are on long-term cortisone, you need to be reminded to take calcium because cortisone thins the bones.

Women who take medication for osteoporosis may not realize they also need to take calcium and vitamin D. If you take more than 600 mg of calcium each day, it is best to take the pills in two separate doses, with food, to ensure that your body absorbs it. If you are taking osteoporosis medicines such as Fosamax® and Actonal® be especially careful about the timing of the calcium doses. Calcium interferes with the body's absorption of these medicines and therefore should be taken at different times of the day.

If you take a lot of medication, your pharmacist can tell you when to take them—with food, after food, mornings, or evenings. There are valid reasons for taking different medications at certain intervals. As we get older, most people take more medications, and it is important to know when to take them and whether they should be taken before, with, or after eating. Food is an important factor because it can interfere with or help the absorption of a drug. Many medications interact with alcohol. When in doubt, ask the pharmacist.

Medical compliance is very important. Some medications need to be taken on a regular basis. Some people skip their medication for a day or two because they are busy, they don't like the side effects, or they can't afford it. It is *vital* that you communicate this to your pharmacist. With some medications, it does not matter, but with others skipping doses can have serious consequences.

Depending on the climate and your mobility, pharmacy delivery service is important if the weather is bad or you can't get out. Check to see if the pharmacy can deliver when you are unable to pick up your medication.

Most drug stores sell beauty products. When buying a moisturizer, get one with a sunscreen protector, in the range of 15 to 35 SPF and use it 365 days of the year. Research has shown that the skin can be damaged even in the winter. Most people use sunscreen for the face only, but we recommend that it also be used on the hands and ears.

When going out of town, ask your pharmacist for advice about how to carry your medicines. All medications should be carried in your hand luggage rather than in a suitcase that can get lost or exposed to extreme temperatures. If you're going on a long car trip, don't store medicines in the glove box or trunk, which can become too warm. If you are going on a five-day trip, take enough medicine for seven to eight days, just in case your trip is extended. The pharmacist can also make other suggestions, based on your medical history and travel destination.

Customers often ask me what they should keep in their medicine cabinet. The following list is useful:

- Pain and anti-inflammatory medicines such as Tylenol and Advil
- Aspirin; apart from its well-known pain relief benefits, aspirin could be used at the onset of a heart attack to prevent blood clots.
- Anti-diarrhea medication
- Calcium or Tums
- Antibiotic ointments
- Antihistamines
- Over-the-counter cortisone cream for rashes
- A mild laxative or stool softener (You can actually have a heart attack if you are constipated too long because of exertion when expelling the stool. So if you have not had a bowel movement for three days, do something!)
- Moisturizing eye drops. As we get older, out eyes tend to be dry; the heating in houses also provokes dry eyes.

- Anti-histamine eye drops (Reading too long or working on the computer can cause red eyes. These drops take out the redness.)
- Cold and cough medicine, like Robitussin DM
- Band-Aids, cotton, strapping bandages for twisted ankle or sprained knee.
- Rubbing alcohol to cleanse a cut or a scratch; especially necessary if you are a gardener and have cuts and scrapes.

Every six months to a year, you should go through your medications to check if any have expired. If they're out of date, toss them out.

YOUR THOUGHTS:

_____

_____

_____

_____

_____

_____

THE FINANCIAL PLANNER

I had always assumed that financial planners were only for the rich. Then a friend told me that after the holidays she had been up to her ears in credit card debt and did not see a way out. She called a financial planner who gave her a step-by-step strategy, and she is now financially stable. I thought it would be useful to know more about how a financial planner can help so I asked Brian Kohute, CPA/PFA, CFA, MST, who is managing partner of HJ Financial Group, a wealth management firm located near Philadelphia, PA.

Most of us are used to a regular income. We are very busy with our day-to-day lives and assume that we will always have an income. We need to take time to project what will happen financially if the steady flow of salary or other income slows or ceases. We assume retirement will be covered by Social Security and pensions, but this just isn't the case any more. It is important to pause and plan our financial future while we have income coming in and are able to plan. This is the time when we could use the services of a financial planner.

As many baby boomers enter a new stage in their life, retirement or "financial independence" as we like to call it, there is a major call or need for women to take more control of their finances whether they are single, married, divorced, or widowed. The question is, how does one take control of her finances?

The first step in any journey is to plan your trip. The retirement journey may consist of a lot of twists and turns, or it may be a straight line. Either way, you need to develop a map for the course you want to take. The expertise of a financial planner can guide you on your journey. Some questions you need to address along they way are:

- How to generate income to live on?
- How to invest so you don't outlive your money?
- What are your true retirement expenses?
- Is your health insurance adequate?
- Do you need long-term care insurance?
- Is your estate plan sound and up to date?
- What can you give to the grandchildren without worrying about running out of money?

Once you have your map sketched out, you need a vehicle to get you there. The vehicle is the process you are going to use to reach your destination, which is a life with the least amount of financial worry. That process is called "financial planning." Do not confuse financial planning with financial products. Financial planning is a process or strategy to help you achieve your goals. Financial products (annuities, for example) may or may not be needed to help you achieve those goals. Financial planning is analysis and number-driven. It is indifferent to any specific financial product. Working with a financial planner can give you the tools you need to choose the products that will help you meet your goals.

What are the dos and don'ts of hiring a financial advisor? The Do's include:

- A referral from someone you trust, whether it is a friend, co-worker, accountant, or attorney.
- Professional designations are preferable: Certified Financial Planner (CFP) or Certified Public Accountant/ Personal Financial Specialist (CPA/PFS).

- Make sure you understand the financial planning process that the financial planner uses and how he or she will be compensated to deliver the services to you. There is no right or wrong method of compensation. The only important thing is to understand what you are paying in fees or commissions and how you are paying the fees.
- Check the background of your prospective advisor. Ask them how to do so; if they are not comfortable telling you how to check them out, they are probably hiding something.
- Ask questions if you don't understand what they are telling you. It may all sound very complicated. But at the end of the day if you don't understand the plan, how will you achieve it?

The Don'ts

- Don't buy any product until you have a financial plan that you understand and are comfortable with.
- Don't buy anything that you don't understand how to get rid of. By that I mean, how long do you need to stay in the product and what cost will you incur to get out of it?
- If someone is offering a great return, with no risk, it is probably a rip off. Anything that sounds too good to be true generally is.
- No one works for free. If anyone tells you that you are not paying for their product or service, run for the door as quickly as you can.
- Insurance is meant to protect you against risk. It is generally not a great investment. Don't buy a lot of insurance at this stage in your life unless you really

need the death benefit for your family or to pay estate taxes.

- Don't be afraid to shop around. Financial planners come in all shapes and sizes; there is no one-size-fits-all. Find one whom you trust and with whom you can have a productive relationship.

Financial planning is simply about setting goals, developing a plan to achieve them, and then executing the plan, monitoring, and adjusting it as required or necessary. Your financial plan should be monitored quarterly, or more often if a major life event occurs, and updated every year or two. Remember, financial planning is about living the life you want, not living a life you feel you have to because you can't afford a better one.

YOUR THOUGHTS:

_____

_____

_____

_____

_____

_____

THE WEIGHT LOSS MOTIVATOR

I know there are more important things in life, but losing weight is important to many of us, either for a better self-image or for health reasons. I therefore asked Penny, a popular weight loss motivator, what she found worked in losing weight after fifty.

I have been a weight loss motivator for ten years. While my clients come to me for weight loss, my concentration is on eating for good health. I do not believe in fad diets. My goal is long range: to teach good eating habits. I don't believe in instant weight loss at the cost of good health. I quote Rochefoucauld who said, "To eat is a necessity, but to eat intelligently is an art." When we abuse our bodies by starving ourselves, we commit a crime against ourselves.

My years of teaching women how to eat well to lose weight have taught me that the difference between success and failure is dependent on four factors:

- *Willingness to make changes*: This is the first step and the hardest. If you realize that whatever you were doing before did not work, you will understand that making changes is essential. Unless you do something different from what you were doing before, nothing will happen. Most people are resistant to making changes because old habits are comfortable.
- A *positive attitude*: Attitude is everything. It is the key to a food plan and everything else in life. You need to feel you are worthy of success. A lot of people do not

feel they are worthy of success and that is the hidden agenda that stops them from keeping the weight off.

- *Willingness to get help*: It is difficult to accomplish goals on your own. Drawing on others for support can keep you going when you are ready to quit. If you don't want to join a group, perhaps you can ask a good friend for support, one who will acknowledge your effort and encourages you with "I know you can do it." If a friend is not available, sometimes a husband or caring child can help. As Goethe said, "Nothing will strengthen a man more than the confidence shown in him."
- *Persistence*: In all aspects of life, persistence makes the difference between those who succeed and those who fail. It is especially true in weight loss.

If these four factors are present, I can accurately predict who will succeed and who will fail. Conversely, if people are not willing to change old habits, if they do not believe they are worthy, if they are not willing to accept help, if they will not pick themselves up and try again, the very high probability is that they will fail. One predictor for failure is "The Blame Game." Blaming friends, family genes, etc., is a way of avoiding responsibility.

I teach my clients to recognize two common pitfalls to weight loss:

- The difficult days when they eat more than they had intended to eat. This leads to the "I blew it today, but I'll start my diet again tomorrow" syndrome that leads to discouragement and backsliding. It's important to learn to be more kind to ourselves. We all make mistakes. We need to accept our imperfections and learn from them.
- Friends or well meaning relatives who insist you have "just one more piece of cake." Plan ahead how to

respond or avoid friends who sabotage you. Try to eat with friends who support your new eating habits.

A key to weight loss, and maintaining a healthy weight, is to be aware of our behavior around food. If we can become more alert to why and where we eat, we can take steps to change our eating behaviors. Some specific steps:

- Drink six to eight glasses of water a day.
- Affirm yourself and your efforts: "Yes, I can. Yes, I can. Yes, I can." You would be surprised at the effectively of affirmations.
- Gaining food knowledge. Knowledge is power: understand nutritional labels.
- Enjoy your food; savor it.

Even though I am a weight loss motivator and have maintained my weight for fifteen years, I still have moments of temptation. Unless I am vigilant, it is easy to let the weight creep back on. I stay on track by listening to other people and how they deal with their temptations. We all have the same problems, and listening to other peoples' success stories helps.

If there is one thing I learned as a weight loss motivator, it's that it all comes down to doing the work. You can eat well, enjoy good food, and succeed, if you are willing to follow the steps to success.

YOUR THOUGHTS:

_____

_____

_____

_____

_____

THE PERSONAL TRAINER

Concerned about osteoporosis, I treated myself to a personal trainer two years ago. It was one of the best things I ever did for myself. Not only did my bone density improve, but it also motivated me to exercise at home. My measurements changed, and I have more energy. I am so happy that Debbie Hufnagel, a certified personal trainer, gave me an exercise regime that works for me. Here is her approach to exercise:

I'll start by telling you a little about my background. I am an AFAA certified personal trainer. I have eight years of personal training experience as well as over fifteen years of group fitness instruction. I specialize in training special populations and often work in conjunction with physical and occupational therapists to design customized workout programs. Everyone is unique. People have different medical and physical needs. I concentrate on safety and injury prevention. At 50+ there is less emphasis on quick fixes and more on healthy lifestyle changes.

My number one goal is to inspire my clients to embrace a healthy lifestyle. Exercise is essential to maintaining health. Not only does exercise help you burn more calories by creating lean muscle mass, it also reduces risks for obesity and diseases such a diabetes and osteoporosis.

Did you know that falling is the number one cause of injury as we mature? It is so important that we increase our balance to prevent falls. Many diverse classes are offered that focus on balance. Just find what motivates you and incorporate it into your routine. If you like to workout out alone, there are many great videos. If you would rather workout with other people, many classes are offered at gyms, churches, or community centers. You can take a yoga class, a Pilate class or Tai chi. Maybe you like pole dancing, absailing or belly dancing. How about a traditional low impact class?

What to wear? Your workout attire should be comfortable and make you feel good. Shoes are CRITICAL! You need shoes that are fitted to your feet and the activity that you plan to do. Running shoes are different from walking shoes. Aerobic shoes are different from cross trainers. If you aren't sure what type of athletic shoes to buy, ask a trainer. Shoes need to be replaced frequently.

Doesn't "reversing the aging process" sound wonderful? Well, it is easy if you do three things: Strength train, cardio train, and eat healthy foods. Studies show that women of all ages can see dramatic improvement in their muscle mass and body fat ratio if they work out regularly and eat correctly.

If you want to hire a personal trainer, this is what to look for:

- Compatibility—You need to get along with the trainer you hire.
- Price—Does it work within your budget?
- Certifications of the trainer—Make sure they meet the needs you are looking for.
- Training philosophy—Be sure your trainer understands your medical needs and goals and can meet them.

We've all heard that phrase, "No pain, no gain." I tell most of my clients, "Yes, you may feel uncomfortable when you are pushed a little to increase your training. That is okay. What is not okay is true pain. You must always listen to your body and stop whenever you feel that an exercise is not appropriate for you."

When working with a personal trainer, be clear and vocalize any suggestions or concerns you have. The result will be a safe and effective workout. So remember, communicate!

YOUR THOUGHTS:

_____

_____

_____

_____

_____

_____

THE MAKEOVER ARTIST

I love watching makeovers on television—seeing a dowdy housewife transformed into a glamorous siren, a plain looking woman turned into a beauty. It's fun and exciting to see the end result. I asked an international makeover artist, Liz E. London, if she could tell me something about her experiences with makeovers and to give us some ideas on how to project our best image.

To me, a makeover is about changing one's image or enhancing what is already there. Your clothes and accessories not only reflect your mood, but they should also be appropriate for the life you lead. They can also be the tools for creating the image you want to convey.

For private clients, including models and public figures, I select clothing and accessories and suggest makeup changes. On television I work with a makeup expert and a top hairdresser. Some results are truly spectacular. A makeover can create dramatic changes in the life of the participants.

One of the most exciting makeovers I ever did was the transformation of a slovenly pub owner into an elegant lady. She was just less than five feet tall, overweight, wore a size twenty dress, and had a large bust. Her face was full, her complexion uneven. To add height to her figure, I selected a royal blue crepe dress with box pleats to create a long line. Long strands of pearls repeated the vertical line. A matching hat added softness and elegance. Her hair was lightened to an ash gray-blonde and styled off her face in an upsweep wave. Cosmetics were applied subtly—concealer under the eyes to eliminate puffiness, contouring with rose-brown blush to reshape her full cheeks, and pink-mauve lipstick to contribute to the overall softness of her new face.

The transformation was amazing. As the makeover progressed, her posture changed. She held herself more erect. She had a wonderful, amusing personality, and her makeover gave her a boost in confidence. This led to her appearing on talk shows and becoming a local celebrity.

Another success story was the changed image of a rather plain looking housewife to a confident, capable, dynamic business executive. Again, this was done with quality clothing, accessories that made an impact, some jewelry (a watch with a leather strap, classic earrings, stick pin, pearls) soft makeup, and a well-groomed hairdo. As a result, she was able to land the job she wanted.

Makeovers do not always have happy outcomes, however. A young grandmother who had not changed her long-hair image since high school but now wanted a new look, was given a pleated camel skirt and long vest that camouflaged her short waist and slimmed her hips. I added a checked Burberry scarf to draw the eye downward and create an illusion of height. Her hair was cut short and swept off her face to give her a more youthful appearance. A warm peach foundation, coral lipstick, and teal blue eye shadow gave her a new more contemporary look. She looked smart and stunning.

When her husband saw the "new woman," he did not like the result. That night as she was asleep, he took the new clothes and threw them in the garbage. He was not comfortable with, or felt threatened by, his wife's new image. He preferred the image he was used to.

Some women were given wonderful makeovers but for one reason or another did not maintain their new look. Having said this, we all want to look our best, to create the illusion of youth, grace, and beauty. And it's never too late to take charge of looking your best for the rest of your life.

Elegance, poise, and posture make the fifty-plus woman stand out in any crowd. It starts with good posture. Posture is the key that every model uses to convey youth and presence. Good posture can make you look ten pounds lighter. Bad posture can make you look ten years older (and *feel it*). Stand tall. Pretend you are holding a coin between your shoulder blades to remind you to keep your back and shoulders straight. If you are willing to take the time to practice, you can convey that very rare ingredient—presence.

To update your look, every five years modernize your makeup and try a new haircut. Keep reinventing yourself. Consider highlighting your hair or wearing a spikier hairdo. When choosing clothing, never buy anything uncomfortable—you won't feel good wearing it. For an elegant and chic look, color coordinate your stockings and shoes with the hem of your skirt. Before leaving the house, take a few minutes to check the back of your hair and the slit in your skirt.

An "old" look is not an asset in business or in private life. Four signs of aging in women are dated makeup, a dated hairstyle, dated glasses, and lipstick that runs into crease lines. Women can age instantly by bad posture (slouching), wearing the wrong undergarments, cheap fabrics, run down shoes, and outdated clothes and accessories. The wrong bra can give you a droopy bust and create bulges in sweaters and clinging clothes. Conversely, the right undergarments can camouflage body flaws and give a much smoother line to your figure. A lipstick pencil can prevent lipstick from running into crease lines.

To appear younger, start by updating last year's wardrobe with this year's accessories, whether it's a large flower on the lapel or a funky handbag or shoes. Mix a tweed jacket with plain trousers or jeans. Don't wear the complete look of one designer; instead add a quirky bit of imagination like putting several broaches on the lapel of a jacket or use a scarf for a belt. Wear colors that are snappy and well-coordinated. Wear your most flattering color next to your face—it can transform your look.

A few tips to enhance your appearance: Avoid harsh or silvery colors on the eyes. Bulky or geometric shaped earrings can improve the less-than-perfect jaw line. Pearls and beads intertwined create a luxurious look. Avoid dull, mousy colors, very blue or purple lipstick, and long dangling earrings that tend to pull the face downward. And to quote from Audrey Hepburn's Beauty Tips: "For attractive lips, speak words of kindness; for lovely eyes, seek out the good in people."

Is there a man in your life who asks your advice on how to update his image? A man wearing a comfy, button down cardigan, flannel shirt, white socks, scruffy shoes, and unfashionable glasses with tan plastic frames automatically conveys an old look. Give that same man a vibrant V-neck sweater in bright blue, red, or lilac. Combine it with white trousers and fashionable deck shoes, and you will transform Gramps into groovy. Or have him try a jacket with a cotton tee shirt instead of a button down shirt, shoes that are shiny and new looking, a crisp show of starched cuff in a dress shirt with a red tie, and dark trousers in a non-shiny fabric. And for a luxurious touch, there is nothing like the soft feel of a man in a roll neck cashmere sweater.

It takes a certain amount of discipline to achieve the image you want, but it's worth it. So take the time to rediscover the "real you" by starting with the external you. Explore more up-to-date clothing and new make-up and hairdos. Dare to be different and, above all, take the time to enjoy life.

YOUR THOUGHTS:

THE COMPUTER COACH

The personal computer and e-mail have drastically changed our lives and communication. Many people over fifty, however, are reluctant to explore this new means of communication. I was one of them. Now that my husband is working less, we have more time for leisure, and exploring what the personal computer has to offer is a new learning experience that we want to do together.

For me and many others over fifty, the Internet has opened new doors for staying in touch with friends and relatives and expanding opportunities to learn new things by web-surfing. I was encouraged to learn that more and more members of our generation are going online. I asked Karen Strauss, owner of Main Street Technology in Narberth, PA. (which specializes in coaching adults to use computers with confidence) to tell us more:

No one is ever too old to learn to use a computer. The oldest person I work with on the computer is ninety one! He says that it keeps his "mind alert," and he is challenged because he has the use of only one eye. I also work with an eighty-year-old woman who has macular degeneration but pays her bills through the Internet.

Here are some reasons to use a computer in this stage of your life:

- Keep in touch with family members.

The Internet has improved our connections with family members. E-mail is the number one draw for seniors. Their prime reason to go online is to connect with children, grandchildren, and friends. Families are scattered all over the globe and are on different schedules. E-mail is an easier (and cheaper) way to keep in touch.

Sylvia, a retired nurse, frequently hears from a granddaughter who does a quick e-mail from her desk during the workday. Another woman hears from her grandson who is studying in Australia; he includes photos. A daughter keeps her mother up to date on daily happenings at her college.

Others take advantage of instant messaging. When people are on the computer, they send notes back and forth. Instant messaging can also take place all over the globe, and is a cost-effective way to stay in touch.

- Get information to be better informed.

People know that they are missing out when every article and TV story says visit us at *www.you-fill-in-the-address.com.* A wealth of current information is available through the Internet on health, finance, and travel.

You can gather information about health from some of the best resources in the country to make you feel more informed about questions you may want to raise with your doctor.

You can also access current financial information instead of waiting for statements to come in the mail. You can travel the world looking at sites, planning travel arrangements from airlines to hotels, and booking tickets.

- Have fun with your hobbies.

Avid bridge players can play against the computer or play with other bridge lovers all over the world. Some people love to research family history through the Internet. There are wonderful resources online that you can visit.

- Shop on the Internet.

Begin with sites of retailers that are well known to you. Look for the information indicating that the sites are secure. They will have an icon with a lock in the lower right corner of your screen and mention that they are "encrypted." This scrambles the information as it travels over the Internet to make personal information, such as your credit card numbers, secure.

There is much more you can do with computers. For example, you can write anything from letters to novels to memoirs using word processing. You can create your own greeting cards. You can even get into the world of digital photography and print pictures or scan and retouch old sentimental family photos.

At first, it may feel intimidating to begin using a computer. A retired executive shared this thought after completing his first computer course: "It is depressing to observe one's grandchildren sitting down in front of a computer and making it perform its miracles while we are still in the elementary phase of education."

You will need to be patient with yourself when beginning to use the computer. Sometimes computers act up, and you need to shut them down for a while rather than feel frustrated. To make your computer learning experience run more smoothly, try out the following suggestions:

- Find someone outside your family to be of help to you.

Every family has a "computer genius," yet they may live too far away, never have time to help, or perhaps when they do help they talk and move too fast. I recommend taking some professionally taught classes. Look for programs in your area that specialize in adults, such as local community programs, senior centers, or libraries. You may even want to hire someone to work with you individually.

- Use caution when going on the Internet.

Use the same precautions that you would use when you are visiting a large city. For example, communicate cautiously with strangers. If you are not familiar with someone who sends you an e-mail, delete it. Do not open any attachments from anyone you do not know. Make sure your computer system has protection from intruders. This includes keeping up-to-date security programs such as anti-virus, firewalls, and spy ware, as well as Windows updates. And most importantly, do not share your social security number with anyone on the Internet.

YOUR THOUGHTS:

_____

_____

_____

_____

_____

_____

THE FENG SHUI PRACTITIONER

A recently widowed friend needed to get the clutter out of her house and mind. She succeeded through feng shui, which made me curious about the potential benefits of this ancient approach to living well. So I asked Roslyn Skversky Squire, a certified national feng shui consultant with over twenty-five years of experience, to explain what feng shui can do.

In its purest form, feng shui is the ancient Chinese art of improving your life through purpose and intention by redirecting the flow of *chi* (energy or inner force that pulses through everything). As a method of integrating our internal and external environments to help affect a personal transformation, feng shui can help us attain our life goals. Each person is a lodestone that attracts energy, including predecessor history—from the walls, furniture, colors, plumbing, traffic patterns—of our surroundings. We also unknowingly project and add our own state of being. The space around us mirrors its previous energy, mingles with our own, beams it into our inner core, and reflects it to the outside world.

Chi provides motion and vitality. In our bodies and our environments, our personal *chi* dictates the overall quality of our lives and the spaces we inhabit. If you sense that your physical surroundings are clogged and cluttered, your ability to think, focus, and act may be adversely affected. If your space is boring, you may experience the "blahs" and feel lethargic or apathetic. If your environment is unwelcoming, your work or social life may be disrupted. Imagine how your own life situations—your career, knowledge, family, wealth, reputation, relationships, communications, support systems, and health might be affected, for better or worse, by your *chi*. Energy can take many forms; it can meander, linger, calm, balance, harmonize, or soothe, depending on your intentions and life circumstances. If you can harness this energy, you will develop a sense of congruency, a potent equilibrium.

Feng shui is not, as many people think, simply about moving furniture or painting walls. The purpose of feng shui is to wed form and function into harmoniously balanced and aesthetically pleasurable interior and exterior living spaces.

Let's use the entryway to your home as an example. Look at the pathway leading to your home. Is this the journey you want to take? When you come home, would you rather be walking into your own house or is it the one down the street that draws you instead? Every entrance fosters a first impression and communicates volumes about who lives inside. Your front door is not just the way you enter and exit your home; it represents the transition from the outer, often frenetic, world into our own inner sanctum. The way you perceive your comings and goings can affect and determine major aspects of the life you live.

Try a little experiment. Walk outside your home and approach it with fresh eyes, as a stranger would. What is your first impression of the main entrance? How does it speak to you? Does it say, "Welcome, come in" or "Back off"? Might visitors be confused as to which is the main entrance? Is your address clearly marked? Is the pathway to your door unobstructed? Is the space well lit? Is your entryway what you want to project to the world? Does it make you feel happy? angry? raring to go?

The entrance to your home is, metaphorically, also the door to your body. In feng shui, we call it "the mouth of *chi*," the way energy enters. The flow should put you at ease. Great care should be taken in nurturing this essential part of your home, your "second skin." Think of *chi* as oxygen. If you breathe deeply and rhythmically, and if the pathway to your lungs is clear, you can take in abundant life-giving oxygen. So it is with the energy of the home. The "mouth of *chi*" allows in or shuts out the life force—opportunity, auspiciousness, luck, or good fortune. You may literally be thwarting and reducing the flow of *chi*. Consider how you could make your entryway more welcoming. Try adding light, widening a walkway, removing obstructions, trimming hedges, cleaning up litter from your yard. Allow your imagination and creativity to roam free—and trust your instincts!

Let me use a case study to show how feng shui can make a difference: I asked a client—I'll call her Ms. A—to decide what she hoped to accomplish. Her goals were to recover more fully from her divorce of five years ago, to reduce generalized chaos and anger in her life, to become unstuck and stop clinging to the past, to decrease stress that had resulted in various bothersome health problems (from frequent colds to lack of sleep to headaches to loss of appetite), and to establish more meaningful communications with her family and friends. This is what we did: We looked at Ms. A's home with "new eyes," using all perceptions available to her. We questioned previous assumptions, assessed her type of personality, redefined her goals, and she set her intentions with sincerity.

Next we performed an "interior blessing," which she and her family designed and fully participated in (after choosing from a variety of well known tangible Feng Shui "enhancements" that I had recommended), to rid their house of detrimental predecessor history. Then Ms. A redesigned the placement of her rooms. She moved her bedroom—dingy, poorly lit, cluttered, and unwelcoming—into her living room, a relatively unused, sunny, well lit space. The living room had previously been used only for show. It already contained many things she loved. We removed any objects associated with unpleasant memories. We positioned her bed so that it faced and was farthest from the door. We redraped her windows, added a favorite antique carpet from storage, hung a few meaningful fabrics and tidbits that she had picked up in her travels, and included her favorite music and books. After she spent only one night in her new bedroom, I noticed that her voice had become stronger and had a lyrical quality to it. The work that we accomplished created a safe container in which energy could more freely move. This begging-to-be-found energy was infusing her surroundings with new harmony, life, and positive forward-moving flow. She then was able to reflect her positive thoughts, her comfort and vitality onto others, and they in turn mirrored it back to her.

It is important to note the process involved here: Ms. A's transformation did not occur overnight. We continually discussed options, her lifestyle, and her inner thoughts while distilling and refining her goals. She did not follow the dictates of feng shui uncritically; not all were applicable to her circumstances. She ultimately emerged from her cocoon, trusting more in her subconscious mind and "gut" with each flap of her newly discovered wings. Ms. A did not completely refashion herself by any means. She simply tapped into the resource of her temporarily submerged creative self. She recaptured her creativity incrementally and accepted it as a treasure for herself and a gift to others.

Ms. A. became at ease with the freedom and ability to direct her energy towards the present and the future.

She began generating and nurturing the kinds of loving, sharing, spiritual, and comfortable relationships—the pulsing life, she had sought. Unfettered, she gradually became more aware of the goodness and the beauty that surrounded her. With her openness to new perceptions, the feng shui process came easily to Ms. A and she was delighted to have this new implement in her toolkit. With a little practice, she became able to intuit additional cures and apply these concepts for much of the inner and outer inventive work that she continued to undertake.

If you want to explore feng shui, many easy-to-understand books are available. But first, I would like to offer some important tips that you can implement on your own, in your home, today!

Declutter: Open up the pathways to new opportunities and possibilities by getting rid of deadwood that is blocking or sapping your energy. This process is two-fold. Clear the spaces you are living and working in. Clear space within yourself.

Change habitual patterns: If you always do what you've already done, you'll get what you always have. Start simply by driving a different route to work, preparing a gourmet recipe, saying hello to a stranger in an elevator, trying a new exercise, even crawling like a baby in your living room to gain a fresh floor-level perspective. And laugh!

Expand consciousness about the sacredness of your spaces: Creating a specific place of solitude where you can let go of daily travails, refresh your soul, listen to your dreams, regain and renew your essence. Give yourself the gift of a place for contemplation, which allows newness, openness, space for clarity, creativity, and peace. Such a place can be a room, a corner, a niche. Bring into this space the things that make you feel at ease—a favorite chair, book, pictures or whatever may enhance your appreciation of yourself and the preciousness of life.

"Smudge" or clear sufficient static from your life for a specific, achievable goal in your mind. Then just do it! It might be calling a new friend, wearing green instead of black, going to the dollar store, seeing three movies in one day, changing jobs, or beginning to resolve a long-standing conflict. Do it!

. According to Professor Lin Yun's nine easy methods of minor additions ("cures") that you can add around the home to change the energy flow, you can enhance light (brightness), sound (pleasant), life (plants, fish tanks), dynamic process (moving items like fountains, windmills), weight (something heavy/grounding), elements of power, color (art, decorative accessories, fabric), fragrances (incense, potpourri, scented candles) and touch (textures: carpets, wall coverings). These are only a sampling of changes you may choose to make. I suggest that you try only a few. Do them with a sincere heart and visualize positively the change actually occurring. Realize that these additions and adjustments are only tools or bookmarks. What makes them effective is how you do them, how strong your intention/ desire and how meaningfully you reinforce them.

YOUR THOUGHTS:

THE ELDER LAW ATTORNEY

Despite all the lawyer jokes in circulation, older people often need specific legal advice. Anne Marie Levin is an attorney whose practice focuses on elder law and estate planning. Her dedication to the practice of elder law is based on her passion to help those who need it the most. I asked her to explain what elder law is:

Elder law is a relatively new field that is dedicated to serve the legal needs of seniors and the disabled. With 70 million baby boomers moving into their golden years, it is no wonder that elder law is one of the fastest growing fields of law. As awareness of elder law grows, so do the numbers of fifty-plus individuals seeking the counsel of elder law attorneys. Elder law encompasses many areas of the law driven by the special needs of the elderly and the disabled including the following:

- Estate planning, including planning for the management of one's estate during life and its disposition on death by use of trusts, wills, and other planning documents
- Will probate; administration and management of trusts and estates
- Disability planning, including use of durable powers of attorney, revocable living trusts, advance healthcare directives (living wills), for financial management and healthcare decisions
- Medicare, and Social Security claims and appeals

- Medicaid applications and planning; asset preservation to avoid spousal impoverishment when a spouse enters a nursing home
- Health and long-term care insurance issues.
- Guardianships and conservatorships
- Long-term care placements in nursing home and life care communities and nursing home issues
- Elder abuse, fraud, and exploitation
- Housing issues and home equity conversions
- Retirement benefits, survivor benefits, and pension benefits
- Health law and mental health law

An elder law attorney focuses on issues that promote a long and independent life. Of paramount importance is preservation of the client's ability to exercise self-determination, autonomy, and independence for as long as possible. Seniors worry about who will handle their financial and health-care matters for them when they can no longer do so themselves. They are concerned about the disposition of their hard-earned assets upon their death and who will take care of a surviving spouse or dependent child. An elder law attorney reviews personal and financial goals and develops a plan to achieve their individual objectives.

While every person has unique financial resources, family relationships, medical conditions, and personal goals and needs, seniors share many of the same concerns. A person confronted with the reality of failing health and increasing forgetfulness is concerned about management of her own financial affairs, payment of bills, and safety in her home. A consultation with an elder law attorney offers her the information and tools that she needs to plan for disability and long-term care.

Disability planning options include the appointment of an agent under a power of attorney to assist in financial matters when an older person is no longer able to do so herself or the creation of a revocable living trust to manage assets during her lifetime if necessary. A healthcare power of attorney allows a senior to appoint someone to make medical decisions for her if she is not able to do so herself. An advance healthcare directive, generally called a "living will," allows the individual to direct whether she wants life-prolonging measures or treatments in an end-of-life situation when there is no reasonable hope of recovery. The choice of a person to act as agent is of utmost importance. This person may be a family member, trusted friend, or professional. For people who have no family or trusted friends, the issue becomes even more significant.

Many long-term care and living options are considered in view of the individual's needs and the resources available to pay the high costs of assisted living and nursing home care, increased medical costs, or in-home care. A senior may be comforted to learn about the benefits available from Medicaid to pay for nursing home costs. If skilled-nursing care is needed, there are ways to preserve assets from being completely spent, to avoid impoverishment of the spouse who remains in the community, or to permit some of the hard-earned savings to benefit children.

The home is often a senior's largest asset. Considerable thought is given to financial, estate recovery, creditor protection, and tax issues in planning the most appropriate disposition of the home in view of the senior's objectives. For someone who is house rich but cash poor, the attorney will review various options of converting the equity in the home to needed cash, including a home equity loan, reverse mortgage, and transfer of the residence while retaining the right to life in the home for life. Age, income and financial needs, medical condition, and personal objectives play an integral part in these decisions.

An elder law attorney reviews wills, trusts, powers of attorney and living wills. More often than not, people either do not have a will or they have one that no longer reflects their wishes regarding the disposition of property after death. Trusts may be recommended to control the distribution of assets after death, particularly in second marriages or when beneficiaries are minors, disabled, or are pursued by creditors. A parent often wonders what will happen to a disabled child when the parent is no longer able to take provide care. A special needs trust may preserve assets for a disabled child, supplement public benefits to which the child is or may be entitled, and appoint a trustee to act not only as a fiduciary, but also as an advocate and friend in the parent's stead. A power of attorney may need to be updated to conform to current legal requirements. If it is older than a few years, it may not be honored for the significant purposes it is intended to serve. An agent appointed years ago may no longer be able to serve due to medical condition, relocation, or death. In order for all of these documents to be effective, they must be reviewed at least every five years, and more often if there are changes in the law or in an individual's circumstances. Planning and beneficiary designations for retirement plans, which often involve complex tax consideration, should also be reviewed by the attorney.

Any person who is concerned about long-term care for an elderly or disabled family member can also seek the assistance of an elder law attorney. Among the many challenges of turning fifty are the changing needs of aging parents. This burden generally falls upon shoulders already weighed down by the education costs of children and the pressures of earning a living and securing their own financial future. The elder law attorney can assist this "middle generation" with its responsibilities and decisions relating to the long-term care options of elderly parents. Guidance is offered regarding available living options and the means of paying for them. Legal tools, such as durable powers of attorney, assist adult children in making financial and health-care decisions for disabled parents. Public and private benefits may help reduce financial and personal burdens that frequently fall upon children and caretakers of the elderly and disabled.

Often a family seeks the advice of the elder law attorney in a crisis situation. An unexpected illness, accident, or the diagnosis of cognitive impairment, such as dementia or Alzheimer's disease, strikes at the heart of every member of the family. An elder law attorney can assist in emergency planning for disability, long-term care, and financial management. While it is always wise to do this planning before a crisis strikes, much can be done to preserve assets and protect the healthy spouse even in a crisis. The guidance of a seasoned elder law attorney can reduce the difficulty of this most emotional time.

An elder law attorney draws from an extensive knowledge of federal and state laws, court decisions, and administrative rulings. He or she keeps informed daily of the constant changes in laws and social climates. Experience and an in-depth knowledge of the intricacies of estate planning, taxation, and financial issues are vital components of quality representation. You'll want to find an elder law attorney who combines knowledge and expertise with heart-felt compassion and care. Often empathy results from life experiences that promote a deep understanding of the fundamental and personal issues that confront the aging. An elder law attorney can help you connect with other elder care professionals such as social workers, home care specialists, psychologists, and county service providers who may be of further assistance.

Some people wonder, "How do I find a qualified elder law attorney?" A good way to find an elder law attorney in your area is through the National Academy of Elder Law Attorneys (NAELA). A complete directory of member attorneys in your city is available at its website *www.naela. com.* Quality referrals may also be obtained from an attorney who has worked with elder law attorneys in your home town and from local agencies such as the Alzheimer's Association, AARP, Area Agency on Aging, the state or local bar association, or the social service department of your local hospital or nursing home. The best referral is often a friend or neighbor who has consulted an elder law attorney in the past and is happy with the experience.

YOUR THOUGHTS:

_____

_____

_____

_____

_____

_____

PART THREE

THE PRE-DEPARTURE LOUNGE

We're nearly at the end—of this book, that is. I wrote it because I wanted to learn more about the art of living from other women over fifty and from experts who can offer advice for living well. This stage of life is not a bad place to be, actually. I arrived here well before departure, which means I have time to reflect, to think. No definite time set for departure, but I like to be early, to be prepared and, in this case, to reflect.

That's one of the nice things about getting older: having more time for yourself. I am so sorry for the young mothers who "have it all" by working, taking care of children and households, but do not have time to breathe.

Now let's see . . . did I take too much luggage? There are some old "should"s that I am ready to discard . . . some old dreams . . . was I ever that young and naïve? . . . They can be taken out.

Did I complete my paperwork before leaving? Yes, I took the time to make a list of my valuables, send a copy to my family and had them tick off what they want. I don't want unpleasant fights about sentimental or material things. I have seen too many cases of family estrangement when dividing the possessions.

And I finally wrote that ethical will that I had been meaning to write for ages, telling about my family and the values they passed on to me. I wonder if it was too preachy? But I want to hand down a sort of heritage, write down the things that are important to me, and even if the kids will say "Oh, Mother!" I bet they'll pass it on to their children if only because it will give them a sense of identity.

Anything else I forgot? Anyone I forgot to forgive? Anyone I forgot to give a hug and kiss to and tell them how much I love them? . . . There's still time . . .

I think I'll look around—look at the pictures and quotations on the walls. Here's a picture of my mother, and underneath the words she always repeated: *"Do good; be good; be happy."* I tried, Mom, I tried. But it's not always easy to be happy. The psychologist, Dr. Ebert, said we have to put the past behind us, but I still miss you, Daddy, Finnie, and Sheila. And Elizabeth (The Fashion Stylist) said the same thing: "You've just got to face it, get on with life and look forward to the future instead of dwelling on the past."

A quote from Helen Keller— *"Life is either a daring adventure or nothing"*—is on the wall beside the photograph of my father. I love that quote because it reminds me of my father, a quiet unassuming family man, who taught me that "adventure" can be anything you make it mean for yourself—from taking a risk to taking a walk and noticing all the wonderful things you never saw before—the shape of a window, the color of the sky, . . . seeing things you never saw before.

And I remember, as a child, his reading to me from "The Ethics of the Fathers." The saying I particularly remember was:

> *"If I am not for myself, who will be?*
> *If I am only for myself, what am I?*
> *If not now, when?"*

At the time I couldn't understand why the first sentence did not read "If I am only for myself, what am I? "Isn't it selfish to think of yourself first?" I asked. My father's answer was not clear. Reading it as an adult now, it makes sense from a psychological point of view—if we take care of ourselves first, we don't have to give from empty. I think the reason that saying stood out in my mind is that women of my generation were taught to give to others before we gave to ourselves, and it's hard to change. That is why I admire Barbara, The Caregiver, who took time for her own needs whenever possible. And surely care given with compassion feels better than love given with resentment.

And look—a quote from George Bernard Shaw, from a 1907 speech in Brighton, England: *"My life belongs to the whole community, and as long as I live, it is my privilege to do for it whatsoever I can. I want to be thoroughly used up when I die, for the harder I work, the more I live. I rejoice in life for its own sake. Life is no 'brief candle' to me. It is a sort of splendid torch which I have got hold of for the moment, and I want to make it burn as brightly as possible before handing it down to future generations."*

That quote could refer to the lives of many women in this book: Lita, The Politician; Fiona, The Antique Dealer; Celina, The Phoenix; Florence, The Optimist; Laurie, The Theatre Producer; and even Ramona, The Survivor. Actually it could apply to just about all of them. What I find interesting is that, while each has a different lifestyle, most live life fully at this stage of their lives.

I like quotations. Sometimes they make me think, so I turned with anticipation to the next quotation on the wall: *"It is not enough to be industrious—so are the ants. What are you industrious about?"*—Henry David Thoreau.

I interpret this quotation to mean: choose priorities or take the time to think about what one needs in life. Sometimes the answer is as simple as asking the question, "What is missing in my life?" This can lead to a new interest, as Jenny The Adventurous Lady, found when she asked that question and came up with the answer: music. This led her to learning how to play the piano and getting subscription tickets to the Metropolitan Opera in New York.

And sometimes the answer requires doing little things that are difficult. In very sad times, it sometimes takes strength just to get out of bed and get dressed. I noticed, when talking to the woman who lost her soulmate that she made sure she was dressed when she opened the door. And the social worker whom I met four months after she lost her husband had taken the time to dress well. It takes effort to get dressed when it's easier to stay in bed. I remember what Celina, The Phoenix, said: that one of the disciplines in acquiring self-confidence is taking the extra few minutes to look nice or presentable. So maybe during the survival periods of life, one needs to start with the little things and go on with one's own coping mechanisms.

And here is one of my favorite quotes, which I try to apply in life:

"It's easy to have wisdom. All you need do is, when you think of something stupid to say, don't say it."—Sam Levenson

"An unexamined is a life not worth living." I mentioned that quotation from Socrates in the Introduction, and now I reconsider it: After a life is examined, maybe it's time to move on, experience life again, and take with me some of the things I learned from these stories. I like what Dr. Ebert, the psychologist said: "Happiness and joy come from involvement with life, involvement with other people, or in activities that have some meaning for us and contribute positively to our lives and the lives of other people." All the women I interviewed who lived fully and well incorporated that philosophy into their lives.

While I still think comfort and a life of ease is good, it can be boring. Other things that these women found essential include mental and physical exercise and cultivating friends. So many talked about the importance of friends in both good and bad times. One lesson I'm going to apply to my own life is to spend more time cultivating friendships. I'm even thinking of forming a club for "women of a certain age" that would meet once a month and discuss issues meaningful to us.

"In the midst of winter, I finally learned that there was in me an invincible summer."—Albert Camus

When I started this journey, I did not believe I had the strength to withstand serious illness or further loss. But after listening to my peers talk about how they survived tragedies in their lives and still managed to retain their zest for living, I feel that if they could do it, I can do it. And if put to the test, I have the advantage of knowing their coping techniques. Hopefully, however, if I follow the preventive measures given by the different specialists in their fields, I will be able to avoid some life threatening illnesses. And in most cases, one usually has the choice of laughing or crying, and I prefer to laugh. My favorite cartoon is a picture of a tombstone on which this epitaph is written: "Laughter is NOT the best medicine." (Sorry, but I found that funny!)

Here's another quote on the wall: *"A man hath no better thing under the sun than to eat, and to drink, and to be merry."*—Ecclesiastes 8:15

Now that I can relate to! The timing is right and not much effort is required. Besides, who am I to disregard a biblical injunction? Life isn't only about how to overcome difficulties. It is about laughing, living well, and enjoying life.

And look at this—an old gramophone with a record in it. My parents had one just like it. I wonder what's on that record. Let's see, how do I start it? Yes, I remember . . . . And I remember this old song that it's playing,

> Enjoy yourself; it's later than you think, ♪ ♬ ♬ ♪
> Enjoy yourself, while you're still in the pink, ♪ ♬ ♪ ♬ ♪
> The years they go, as quickly as a blink, ♬ ♪ ♬ ♪
> Enjoy yourself, enjoy yourself, ♪ ♬ ♬ ♪
> It's later than you think. ♪ ♬ ♪ ♬

And maybe that's what the art of living is all about—making the best of life and living it fully. That's what I'm going to do, as best as I can.

I want to thank you for joining me on my journey. I hope you have enjoyed meeting these wonderful women and benefited from their life stories as well as from the expert helpers' information. Good-bye and good luck.

Fondly,

Anne

P.S. Do let me hear from you if the experiences of these women have made a difference in your life. You can contact me at **annehadams@comcast.net**.

www.ingramcontent.com/pod-product-compliance
Lightning Source LLC
Chambersburg PA
CBHW061348280526
45784CB00001B/180